I have had the pleasure of attending several of Dr. Norris' seminars and workshops on conflict resolution. Dr. Norris is a dynamic speaker who readily engages his audiences with his humor and his use of practical, real-life scenarios. His new book, *A Tale of Two Perspectives*, is an expanded version of his seminars and workshops, and it is just as engaging and entertaining! This book includes many interesting examples of conflict to which we all can relate. It also provides answers about why conflict occurs and how conflict can be resolved. As a psychologist, I was particularly impressed with Dr. Norris' insightful comments on the behavioral and cognitive patterns that impact conflict and conflict resolution. We all experience conflict from time to time in our personal and professional lives. Some of us work as professionals who assist people engaged in conflicts of one kind or another. *A Tale of Two Perspectives* comes highly recommended. Dr. Norris' book would be extremely useful and beneficial reading for anyone, including the lay public and those who work in the helping professions.

Lisa Varner, PhD
Licensed Psychologist

This book is like a covered bridge between interpersonal conflict and reconciliation. That bridge is girded with sound conflict resolution tools, and covered with divine biblical narratives that provide us with over-arching affirmations during our traverse to peace.

The blending of business issues with skill based and spiritual resolution strategies is a unique and refreshing approach that is useful in the workplace, community, and within families.

These two perspectives are wonderfully interwoven, which create a delightful, substantive storytelling experience that includes practical skills.

Sandra R. Farray, M.A., CPLP
M.A. Conflict Resolution

Certified Professional in Learning
and Performance

It is inconceivable that there is hardly anyone who has not had more than a modicum of experience with conflict. This is true both among individuals and nations. As the author has written, "Conflict is one of those peculiar concepts few people can define without a dictionary, but most people know it when they see it." In his book, *A Tale of Two Perspectives*, Ken Norris has interestingly and informatively drawn insights from secular society and from the richness of his earlier experience as a pastor. The reader will gain a clearer understanding of conflict, its inevitability and an appropriate response. The final chapter alone will make the purchase of the book worthwhile.

Dr. Flynn T. Harrell, Former Executive Assistant to South Carolina's Attorney General, Moderator of Trinity Presbytery, Presbyterian Church (USA) and past President of the South Carolina Baptist Convention

A Tale Of Two Perspectives

Dynamics of Interpersonal Conflict from a Christian Point of View

By

Dr. Kenneth R. Norris

"First be reconciled to your brother"

Humanity travels a collision course with conflict, so it's best to be prepared for the ride.

authorHOUSE®

Ken

10-9-11

AuthorHouse™
1663 Liberty Drive
Bloomington, IN 47403
www.authorhouse.com
Phone: 1-800-839-8640

First published by AuthorHouse 9/1/2010

ISBN: 978-1-4520-5611-1 (sc)
ISBN: 978-1-4520-5612-8 (hc)
ISBN: 978-1-4520-5613-5 (e)

Library of Congress Control Number: 2010910534

Printed in the United States of America

This book is printed on acid-free paper.

Scripture quotations from the Revised Standard Version of the Bible, copyright 1952 [2nd edition, 1971] by the Division of Christian Education of the National Council of the Churches of Christ in the United States of America are used by permission. All rights reserved.

In Loving Memory
Gerald R. Norris

TABLE OF CONTENTS

1. Brussels Sprouts and Other Leafy Green Vegetables 1
2. Have You Been Shopping Only for Apples? 13
3. Fertile Ground for Conflict 23
4. Some Images Are More Divine Than Others 31
5. Toast Sweat and Other Annoyances 37
6. Thou Shalt Not 41
   Substantive Conflict
7. If You Had Been Here! 45
   Relationship Conflict
8. As Simple as A-B-C 51
9. Symptoms of Conflict 61
10. Personalities 73
11. Communication 83
12. Attitudes 91
13. Even Christians Get Angry 97
14. Sometimes Solutions Are Outside the Boat 107
15. The Strategies 115
16. A Misunderstood Strategy 125
17. Say a Little Prayer for Me 131
18. The Ancient Hills Conflict 137
19. Sticks and Stones 145
20. Calculated Forgiveness? 151

ACKNOWLEDGEMENTS

The completion of this manuscript is the fulfillment of a personal and professional dream, spanning several decades. However as it becomes a reality, I am increasingly aware it has not been a solitary journey.

Through the years, my mother has demonstrated how interpersonal conflict is about behavior not people. She has loved me, when I felt most unlovable. She has forgiven the unforgiveable and has never failed to be an expression of God's grace in my life.

My wife, Teri, has graciously sacrificed time that was rightfully hers, so I could fulfill my dream. She has patiently read page after revised page. She has been a consistent source of inspiration, encouragement and insight. I am eternally grateful for her abiding love.

My daughters, Kirstin and Megan, have been the unintentional source of sermon illustrations, newsletter and magazine articles for decades. They are also the source of my deepest and most profound love. They will forever be a part of who I am.

My brother Keith, the prodigal son, remains my friend and advocate. Our lengthy discussions of theology and relationships have fueled my determination to complete this project.

A considerable debt of gratitude is expressed to the individuals whose stories have been compiled into this manuscript. Many of their faces are indelibly inscribed in my memory. Hopefully their experiences will enable others to face conflict with new insights and greater confidence.

PREFACE

After years of graduate and post-graduate research, personality analysis, conflict mediation, developing and teaching workshops on interpersonal conflict, it is still nearly impossible to get it right all the time! Nobody does-not all the time. Interpersonal conflict is hard work and the most critical dynamic is the human equation. It refuses to be taken for granted or predicted, especially when important relationships are at stake.

I have come from a profession in which you could be fired, not only for what you said or did, but for what you thought! You could lose not only your income and reputation, but also your home and your identity. I was a Southern Baptist pastor. Through the decades, my environment has changed, but the interpersonal dynamics have not. People still insist on being unique and where two or three are gathered together, there is bound to be a difference of opinion.

This manuscript is the result of many years of research and personal experiences as a pastor, hospital chaplain and business executive. However, interpersonal conflict, if nothing else, is personal. The anecdotal stories are used to illustrate the dramatic complexities of conflict, but are not intended to cause embarrassment or further exacerbate the consequences. Therefore, names are changed and in some cases, circumstances have been altered to protect the sensitivity and anonymity of the participants.

A Tale of Two Perspectives explores the dynamics of interpersonal conflict from a Christian point of view. However, these insights have been used interchangeably as a guide for the church, home, and modern business. Regardless of whether the objective is improved productivity, harmony in the workplace, civility around the dinner table, or koinonia, the priority must be reconciliation and improved relationships. Jesus said, "First, be reconciled to your brother." After that, you never can tell!

This body of work incorporates biblical narratives and modern techniques into a general resource for interpersonal conflict resolution, from a Christian perspective. The reader is invited to use relevant chapters or larger sections for coping effectively with unique or recurring conflict. Interpersonal conflict can be deeply personal. Please allow this book to be your personal guide.

KRN

ONE

BRUSSELS SPROUTS AND OTHER
LEAFY GREEN VEGETABLES

Siblings will rival. Relatives will drop in and stay too long. Defiant children will demand to know "Why?" Interpersonal conflict is seldom as intense as two gunslingers glaring at each other from ten paces at High Noon. It is seldom as colorful as a red-faced husband and wife, standing in their kitchen, shouting insults. It is more often a tale of two perspectives demanding to be heard.

During my early years in ministry, our little congregation experienced a baby boom of unprecedented proportions. The new church year was only a few weeks away and we were unprepared for the expanding needs of our Preschool Department. Like most churches, we formed a committee.

Jane, the newly elected Preschool Coordinator, promptly reported the purchase of tape recorders for each classroom. I was pleased to see our Preschool needs met so efficiently. It appeared my insightful leadership had paid great dividends!

Later that day, I received a call from Valerie, the new Steering Committee Chairperson. Apparently, she also noticed the Preschool Department's need for tape recorders. She had sent her daughter-in-law to the nearest discount super store with a fist full of cash. Suddenly you couldn't walk through the Preschool Department without stumbling over boxes of tape recorders!

Now, you might think the simple alternative would have been to return some of the tape recorders. That wasn't going to happen!

Valerie announced, "Technically the new year doesn't start until the *first Sunday* in October, so Jane had no right to buy new tape recorders!" Jane said she *officially* went to work on October 1 and had to prepare the department for its first Sunday, so her actions were perfectly justified. How *technical, official* and *justified* we were!

Finally, the daughter-in-law, who bravely risked life and limb at the discount super store, dropped by my office. She said, "I know I'm just being petty, but I'm not going to return those tape recorders. Jane will have to take hers back!" After a brief pause, she gave me a stern look and added, "Ken, I'm going to get my way on this!"

Conflict is one of those peculiar concepts few people can define without a dictionary, but most people know it when they see it! We also want it resolved promptly and to our personal satisfaction. Our little church began its new year with freshly painted rooms, new furniture, energetic Sunday school teachers, excited children and a tape recorder in every Preschool classroom-with eight more stacked in my office!

Afterwards, I became intimately familiar with the irreverent paraphrase of Matthew 18:20: *For where two or more are gathered together, there is bound to be a difference of opinion.* I still recall the defiance in the daughter-in-law's voice as she declared, "I know I'm just being petty, but....I'm going to get my way on this!"

How should Christians resolve interpersonal conflict? Should we simply give in to someone with whom we disagree just to avoid conflict? What are the rules when Christians become petty, insensitive or argumentative? If we love our neighbor as we love ourselves, how do we confront conflict without compromising our values? The solution is to understand and learn to confront the *behavior*, not the *people* we love.

Literally, *conflict* comes from a Latin word meaning to strike. Its definition implies competition, incompatibility, quarrelling, antagonism, internal demands, and even fighting. The catch is that some *strikes* are more destructive or personal than others. For those who need a working definition, let's use this one:

> *Conflict is the experience of individuals or groups who are trying to achieve goals or reach objectives, which are or appear to be incompatible.*

The phrase, *appear to be,* is key to understanding conflict because many conflicts are the result of perceptions and not facts. Of course, most people consider their perceptions factual until proven otherwise.

Conflict is a generic term. It may refer to something as global and complex as peace in the Middle East. It may be as personal as your reaction while sitting in a movie theater, holding hands with your date, after paying twenty dollars for tickets and another fifteen for refreshments, and the light from someone's cell phone rudely breaks the darkness.

Conflict may be as simple as the annoying sound of the alarm clock while realizing you are not ready to face the day. It may be as simple as deciding to wear the red tie or the blue one or to eat corned beef, pastrami or the low fat yogurt. It may be as complex as trying to understand your teenage daughter, who just ran from the room in tears. It might be as benign as rushing through a familiar traffic light on your way to work. It may be as physically upsetting as seeing flashing blue lights in your rear view mirror, with the sudden awareness the traffic light had turned red! Like it or not, human nature tends to travel a collision course with conflict. It is everywhere and easily perceived as bad, harmful or even sinful. So we need to understand it.

We read self-help books. Insightful businesses and churches have workshops to address it. Productive strategies are needed to control it and resolve it, so it doesn't control us! However, most people don't really consider strategies for resolving conflict. Usually, we barge right in, playing out familiar old scripts or memories from our past, hoping things turn out better this time. You might say, we are the product of our memories.

These old scripts are familiar to everyone. Our little dog, Riley, serves as a great example. We have two pugs, Tess and Riley. Tess, the older of the two, is the little black *runt of the litter* my wife Teri carefully selected. Tess sleeps in our bed, sits snuggly under my arm as we watch TV and has seldom heard a harsh word. I jokingly encourage Teri to write her a stern note when she does something naughty.

Riley has lived a different life. We found him in a pug rescue shelter. He came from a family who did not want him. He suffered from heartworms and barely survived. When he arrived at our home, he was a skinny little fawn-colored pug, with a big head, bad manners and a painful history.

Within a few months, Riley began to adjust to his new surroundings. He followed Tess everywhere and still sleeps with his chin on her back. He learned to "sit" and goes to the back door when it is time to do his business, instead of using the furniture. He grew fatter with each day and more accustomed to being loved.

Tess and Riley love to supervise while I cook. They generally sit just far enough away so I won't step on them, but close enough to catch any morsels aimed their way. One night while Tess, Riley and I prepared dinner, Teri became annoyed by a housefly on one of the kitchen curtains. It had to go! Intending not to miss anything, Riley and Tess carefully watched me with one eye and Teri with the other as she opened the closet door. As soon as she picked up the fly swatter, Riley ran!

Not unlike a cartoon character, his short stubby legs seemed to be spinning out of control as his fat little body slid around the corner, down the stairs, into the bedroom and under the bed. Of course, Teri did not intend to hit him, but his tormented little mind was playing an old script. It said fly swatters punish bad little pugs. Clearly, he did not intend to wait around to find out what he had done!

An old adage says if a wise man goes to the refrigerator and finds the milk has spoiled, he does not return a few hours later expecting it no longer to be spoiled. Riley had learned that lesson well. A fly swatter had always meant trouble and the old familiar scripts seldom lead us to new results. The faces may change, but the consequences tend to be just as frustrating as in the good old days. This is because when serious conflict surfaces, we tend to *react* and not *respond*.

A *response* comes from a strategy designed to address the circumstances, personalities and extenuating factors of a particular conflict. It takes time, commitment, understanding and expertise to do this on the spot, so keep reading!

A *reaction* tends to be a knee-jerk action or comment based on emotions or a very familiar script. It's like when you are spending a quiet evening in your favorite chair, drinking a cup of hot tea, reading a magazine article as a moth strays from under the lampshade. Suddenly, it flutters just above eye level. You are startled and swat frantically, causing your glasses to fly across the room!

As an unexpected conflict ignites, especially if it stirs much emotion, we seldom have or allow ourselves time for analysis. We seldom stop to consider the effectiveness of our past strategies. We swat away with all our might to rid ourselves of the little beast. However, if a similar reaction previously resulted in the purchase of an expensive new set of frames, we might soften the blow. We may actually inconvenience ourselves to retrieve the most effective tool: a fly swatter. Just be sure Riley isn't in the room! It works the same way with conflict. Experience, insight and the correct methods will bring increased effectiveness.

A LITTLE CHILD SHALL LEAD THEM

When conflict becomes stressful, it often helps to look back in time. Frequently, conflict returns us to our childhood and how we learned to handle adversity. We may expertly deflect it with humor or hide it with a heavy coat of sophistication, but more often than we want to admit, our little child inside is stomping its feet, holding its breath, demanding to be heard.

It may be helpful to ask, what did conflict look like when I was a child? How did it sound? How did it feel? Was conflict handled calmly and respectfully? Was it more often loud and frightening? Sometimes these answers may help us better understand what issues cause conflict to be personally stressful.

What do the old scripts sound like? Try to recall how parent-child conflicts sounded in your childhood. Were they most often resolved with phrases like: "Because I said so!" or "Don't make me tell you again" or "Stop crying or I'll give you a reason to cry"? The same impatience may filter into relationships later in life, influencing our style of parenting, managing, teaching or supervising.

Another provocative script, "If you loved me you would [fill in the blank]," resonates with many couples in conflict. However, its expectation of a romantic quid pro quo cannot dispute the fact that I may really love you, even cherish you, and still not realize you need or want me to [fill in the blank]. This script often leads to unmet expectations and deep, persistent frustration.

Some of our scripts are familiar, while others are powerfully unique and personal. The old script often quietly rests in a reservoir of childhood memories, until conflict stirs it from its nap. Then like a grumpy three year old, holding his blanket and rubbing his sleepy eyes, a familiar script is about to be heard.

BRUSSELS SPROUTS AND OTHER LEAFY GREEN VEGETABLES

This is not to say conflict is always emotional. Take the matter of brussels sprouts. Apparently, most of us either like them or hate them, but very few of us are on the fence. Conflicting opinions are present, but few of us care! You seldom hear provocative conversations at the water cooler about their savory, versatile flavors. You seldom see folks swapping brussels sprouts recipes in the Break Room. It seems no matter whether you are in Berkley, Birmingham, Buffalo, Boston, Baltimore, or the Bronx, you rarely see much conflict over brussels sprouts!

Conversely, have you wondered why the old adage reminds us never to talk in mixed company about politics or religion? Our perspectives on religion and politics are often intensely personal and very sensitive subjects. They come from places deep within a well-defined value system, creating who we are. We don't like it when our values are challenged. Try discussing abortion, gun control, race relations, and global warming at your next neighborhood cookout.

This may also demonstrate why marital conflicts become so volatile over issues like money, infidelity and failed communication, but rarely over baseball scores or movie reviews. It explains why a teen will defiantly lock herself in her room over not being allowed to drive the family car, but could not care less about the latest downturn in the stock market. Compared to issues attached to our personal value systems, brussels sprouts are relatively unimportant, unless mercilessly linked to a childhood plagued by the *forced* consumption of leafy green vegetables! Then, let the childhood scripts begin. "Eat your vegetables." "You'll get no dessert until you eat your vegetables!" "You can't go outside until you eat your vegetables!" "Okay, just sit there until you eat at least one!"

A PROBLEM OF BIBLICAL PROPORTIONS

Since conflict is so familiar to the human equation, maybe that explains why so much conflict is in the Bible. The Bible brings us into the arena of inter-personal and intra-personal conflict at many turns.

Intra-personal conflicts are intensely personal. They are internal conflicts, often experienced as racing or anguished thoughts or intense emotions, like a broken heart. They cause anxious, sleepless nights. They weigh heavily, sometimes causing uncharacteristic irritability or distraction. They may draw us to an open refrigerator in the middle of the night, put an adult beverage or prescription drug in our hand or take us deeply into our personal Gethsemane.

Some intra-personal conflict in the Bible is obvious, while other instances are gleaned between the lines. We can't avoid being drawn into Jesus' grueling spiritual conflict in the Garden of Gethsemane. The Gospel narratives poignantly describe Jesus as "sorrowful, even unto death" and "greatly distressed and troubled." Some translations mournfully indicate, "His sweat became like great drops of blood."

Other examples include Pontius Pilate obsessively trying to wash Jesus' blood from his hands. We collectively hear the rooster's third and ultimate reminder of Peter's cowardly denials. We can almost feel the flushing of his face, his quickened heart rate and the tightness in the pit of his stomach.

One of the most provocative statements of intra-personal conflict came from the helpless father of a child tormented by a spirit (Mark 9:14-29). No matter whether you believe the boy was possessed by a spirit or suffered from a form of epilepsy, imagine the anguish of the father who watched powerlessly for years as his child suffered relentless seizures. Imagine the deep sadness in his tortured soul as he stood before Jesus and uttered, "I believe; help my unbelief."

As a hospital chaplain, I have heard these troubled words softly echoing from family to family in intensive care waiting rooms. The words may not have been exact, but the sorrowful merging of faith and doubt was very much the same. It called not only for healing, but understanding and grace.

On a lighter note, have you noticed how names sometimes cause internalized conflict? Children with traditional names sometimes shorten them to make them sound cooler, such as changing Charles to Chuck, Lawrence to Larry, Elizabeth to Betty, Bartholomew to Bart. Celebrities also like to play name games, apparently without giving much consideration for how life might be when the child reaches middle school. Nicholas Cage named his son Kal-El after Superman. Gwyneth Paltrow and Chris Martin named their daughter Apple, after, well you know. Imagine what internal conflicts must have plagued Isaiah's son each time he filled out a loan application, in a day without word processors or ballpoint pens, having to write a name like "Mahershalalhashbaz."

Interpersonal conflicts occur between two or more people. This is conflict between husbands and wives, parents and children, bosses and employees. It may be as fierce as a fistfight or a baseball manager screaming in the face of an umpire. It may be as detached as a computer chess match between two ardent rivals in separate cities. It may be triggered by a disagreement over dinner plans, two drivers dashing for a single parking space or two highly motivated warriors with automatic weapons in Afghanistan.

Sometimes our *intra-personal* battles spill over into someone else's world, transitioning into *interpersonal* conflict. For example, dieting tends to be an intra-personal conflict. A prescribed menu of salad and a plain baked potato conflicts with a preferred menu of steak, a loaded baked potato, and pie a` la mode. It becomes *interpersonal* conflict when you fork the hand that reaches to remove the slice of pie from your plate! This difficult transition is also familiar to individuals trying to stop smoking, drinking or consuming caffeine.

The Scriptures dramatically display the churning intra- and interpersonal conflicts in the life of King David. His many struggles with King Saul and his famous clash with Goliath helped build a legend. His affair with Bathsheba, the loss of a child, his guilt, his suffering, and his redemption are all on vivid display.

Interpersonal conflicts tend to make juicy fodder for tabloids, television and movies. Dramas, situation comedies and even 24-hour news channels would hardly reach their respective audiences without an endless supply of interpersonal conflict to keep things lively. Have you noticed how the world audience is so easily drawn to the edge of its seat to watch legal proceedings and interpersonal disputes surrounding O. J. Simpson, Michael Jackson, Anna Nicole Smith and countless unfaithful politicians?

Cain and Abel also quickly come to mind. Two brothers with obvious differences and yet biblical scholars still debate what really went wrong. Jacob's deceitful ploy to deprive Esau of Isaac's blessing also demonstrates a painful extreme of family conflict. Other examples include: confrontations between Moses and the Egyptian Pharaoh over the fate of the Israelites, Elijah's battle with Queen Jezebel, King Nebuchadnezzar's feud with Daniel, confrontations between Paul, Festus and Felix, and of course the ugly turn of events between King Herod and John the Baptist.

Conflict complicated by group dynamics is even more fascinating. Moses faced almost constant interpersonal conflict as the ancient Israelites left Egypt and traveled to the Promised Land. "What should we take with us?" "What are we going to eat?" "How are we going to get everybody across this water?" "Don't we need to stop and ask someone for directions?" "We need a god we can see and touch and worship, like this neat Baal calf!" "Are we there yet?"

Seventeen-year-old Joseph was his father's favorite son! He was also handsome, smart, fashionable and a source of frequent irritation to his brothers! Family dynamics may not always result in selling the offender into slavery, but they carry the potential for passionate disagreements, abuse or alienation.

Emotions like fear, anxiety, forsakenness, shame, and despondency do not have to be found in the Bible to be very real and personal. They smack us in the face every day! It doesn't matter if you carry a Bible, a frying pan or a shovel, conflict may be intensely personal. It also threads its way through the fabric of the church. The church itself has been little more than a microcosm of the conflict playing out in our homes, businesses, ballparks, bus stations and freeways.

During the first decade of the Christian church, Peter, Paul, Barnabas and James took on the religious elite in Jerusalem, demanding inclusion of everyone who accepted Jesus Christ as Savior. The church was still an infant, but conflict was reaching international proportions. Even though the Jerusalem Christians may have had good intentions, Paul and Barnabas knew people were being excluded because they were different.

Apparently, this has not improved with the passing of time. Cheerleaders with bouncy hair, beautiful smiles and contagious personalities exclude introverted, plus-sized girls with glasses and bad skin. Popular, muscle-bound athletes push aside geeks with calculators and pocket protectors. This happens in Sunday school and high school.

Sometimes we exclude people for what they think or believe or how they vote, because of the color of their skin, their marital status or their sexual orientation. This type of very personal conflict is very hard to resolve and often has lasting repercussions.

In Acts, the Hellenists and the Hebrews intensely divided the early church. Differences involved personal and group priorities for their church. These conflicts still surface over things like spending money for a mission trip, a new church van or tape recorders (Think DVD players today). We disagree over whether to start a soup kitchen or buy land for a new sports complex and family life center. However, the differences between the Hellenists and the Hebrews grew increasingly intense and took on a life of their own! They eventually led to catastrophe.

A review of history indicates the Church has not experienced much healing. The Roman Catholic Church has contended with all sorts of conflict. The security of Jerusalem and the Holy Land brought centuries of conflict between Christians and Muslims with the Crusades. Insolent theologians like Martin Luther implied Church doctrine had lost its biblical integrity. Galileo and Copernicus dared introduce science into the religious discussion and Henry VIII's love life stirred frequent conflict with the Pope.

The Protestants did not fare much better. John Calvin's followers became known as Presbyterians after the Scottish Reformation, but even before they could convert their first Native American, they became so doctrinally splintered they were known affectionately as *The Split P's.*

The Episcopalians, who trace their origins to the Church of England and the 16th century conflict between Henry VIII and Pope Clement

VII, usually tend to stay under the media's radar. However, in 2009, about 70,000 conflicted traditionalists formally separated themselves, forming a rival national church.

The Baptists, with whom I share my heritage, seem happiest when in conflict. Through the centuries, this persistent group has managed to survive all sorts of internal conflict, remaining the country's largest Protestant denomination. Each Baptist congregation is autonomous and unique. This independence has led them down many colorful paths of orthodoxy.

A church calling itself *Baptist* should be more specific. Are they Separate Baptists, Armenian Baptists, Free Will Baptists, Landmark Baptists, Primitive Baptists, Northern or Southern Baptists (imagine how they got started), National Baptists, Progressive Baptists, or Two-Seed-In-The-Spirit-Predestinarian Baptists? Even the prestigious Southern Baptist Convention has faced dramatic internal conflict over doctrine and power, resulting in the organization of the Cooperative Baptist Fellowship.

Through the years, the subject matter may have changed, but the intensity and nature of conflict has not. The dynamics of interpersonal conflict can be very challenging and sometimes as familiar as old television reruns. They are also almost always very personal. Consequently, wherever two or three are gathered together, it's best to be prepared!

TWO

HAVE YOU BEEN SHOPPING ONLY FOR APPLES?

For everything there is a season, and a time for every matter under heaven: A time to be born and a time to die, A time to plant and a time to pluck up what is planted; A time to kill and a time to heal; A time to break down and a time to build up; A time to weep and a time to laugh.

Self awareness is a key ingredient in learning to manage and resolve conflict. If I don't understand me, I'm likely going to have an even harder time understanding you! I should know more about me than you, so that seems a better place to start. Self awareness begins with examining why we think like we do. What gives us the perspective we bring to each situation? Charles Dickens wrote:

It was the best of times, it was the worst of times; it was the age of wisdom, it was the age of foolishness; it was the epoch of belief, it was the epoch of incredulity; it was the season of Light, it was the season of Darkness; it was the spring of hope, it was the winter of despair; we had everything before us, we had nothing before us; we were all going directly to Heaven, we were all going the other way....

Our perspective on topics ranging from politics and religion to baking, physics or car repair is limited to our personal frame of reference. This fascinating reality directly impacts our ability to resolve conflict efficiently. "It was the best of times, it was the worst of times," declares the essence of interpersonal conflict: a tale of two clashing perspectives. Charles Dickens no doubt received his inspiration from the words of Ecclesiastes.

Our frame of reference influences our perspective on any particular issue. But having a limited frame of reference is like slipping into a movie twenty minutes after it has started. You may have a basic understanding of the plot, but your perspective is limited. You have no frame of reference to indicate where you are in the story.

Our frame of reference is created and reshaped throughout life. It is sculpted by memorable events, accomplishments and failures, our parents, teachers, Sunday school teachers, pastors, Scout troop leaders, co-workers, neighbors, geographic location and the media. Newspaper editorials, magazine articles, books, radio and television shows all help create a frame of reference which colors our perspectives on just about everything.

At age twenty-one, we thought we were invulnerable, bullet-proof! We did not need car seat belts to restrain our freedom or health insurance to consume dollars needed for pizza, gasoline and adult beverages. At sixteen, we perceived thirty-five as ancient! At thirty-five, the new mile marker mystically transformed into fifty! When sixty came along, we simply declared it "the new fifty."

Geography also influences our frame of reference. Try offering a bowl of grits to someone visiting Charleston, South Carolina from Buffalo, NY. After he makes the awful face, tell him it is polenta. Invite a lifelong resident of Mt. Airy (Mayberry), North Carolina to New York City and tell him to take the subway from Queens to Battery Park.

Our frame of reference helps define our perspective, but everyone does not have the same frame of reference. The potential for conflict arises when people have opposing perspectives or simply do not understand each other.

Imagine you have been dieting for several weeks in anticipation of a Florida vacation. Living on a thousand calories a day, you walked an hour a day and managed to lose about twenty pounds. You still have a few pounds to lose, but you are finally ready for the sun! While packing your suitcase, you can't help glancing into the mirror, admiring your new and improved body.

Finally in sunny Florida, you dress in your new smaller sized swim suit and make your grand appearance on the hotel swimming pool deck. Careful to ensure everyone gets a meaningful glimpse of your new figure, you casually glide around the pool, searching for just the right deck chair. Here's the problem. No one seems to notice your bold accomplishment. You are just another sunbather with a few pounds to lose. No one knows about your weeks of sacrifice or the twenty pounds you have already lost. No one cares. They have no frame of reference from which to recognize your accomplishment. They've not seen you before that moment.

Stop what you are doing. Look around your present environment very slowly. Carefully study everything. Pay close attention to every detail. If you are in a room, notice the drapes, chairs, light fixtures, books, lamp shades, wall covering, carpet and the exit signs. If you are outside, notice parked cars, traffic lights, or pedestrians. Notice the leaves, children's attire, Frisbees, balls, dolls, swing sets, and dog collars. Notice shirts, blouses, socks, and hair color. Wherever you are, make a precise *mental* note of everything nearby that is *red*. You may want to get a slip of paper and something with which to write for later. Do not start your list yet!

How do you feel about Good Friday or prayer in the school? What do you think about politicians? How do you feel about people who receive welfare or use other government assistance programs? What do you think about people who drive gas-guzzling pick-up trucks or hybrids? How do you feel about police officers? Someone who received a speeding ticket last week will likely feel differently than someone who has never received a ticket or recently called the police after a home burglary. These and similar questions help define our frame of reference.

Our frame of reference is broadened with new experiences and as we invest ourselves in particular issues and interests. I will have a broader frame of reference if I have actually cooked Coq a vin, than if I have only read about it in a cookbook. Someone who enjoys watching from a porch swing as the moon drifts slowly across the evening sky will have a different perspective than someone who studies it through a telescope. Astronaut Neil Armstrong will have an even broader frame of reference. All three will have different perspectives.

If I listen to speeches, analyze debates, read newspapers and consider many different perspectives, my judgment about an election will be more informed, than if I adopt the perspective of a popular radio talk show host. A broader frame of reference allows us to see different perspectives and make better decisions. It opens our eyes to alternatives or unexpected solutions, not readily apparent to individuals with less perspective. It is a critical tool in learning to respect and appreciate others.

Becoming effective in interpersonal conflict resolution requires a perspective broad enough to understand the perspectives of others, even when they seem a little far-fetched! So, how do you think your perceptions have changed through the years? What experiences have broadened or narrowed your perspective?

As a child in the fifties, I selected my favorite television shows from only three local stations and had to get out of my chair to change the channel. Today, we have hundreds of channels from which to choose and nobody gets up to change the channel anymore. As a teen, I thought it really cool for someone to have a telephone in their car. Today, cell phones, Blue Tooth technology, iPods and texting are part of everyone's daily commute. Do you define success and failure in the same terms you once used? Have you become less threatened and more tolerant of differing opinions?

An individual reared in a home where conflict took the shape of verbal, emotional or physical abuse will likely view conflict differently than someone who saw it resolved with calmness and mutual respect. An individual whose parents celebrated successes, but also empathized with failures, will respond differently to adversity than one who was sharply chastised or alienated for simple mistakes. A child maturing with realistic parental expectations will have different concepts of success and failure than one whose parents never accepted anything less than perfection or winning at all cost.

Someone who saw her parents forced to use segregated water fountains, restrooms, movie theaters and doctor's offices, will have a different perspective of Barack Obama's presidency than someone who grew up under the security of Civil Rights legislation. The broader frame of reference belongs to the one who actually saw the injustices and felt the sting of humiliation and bigotry. From childhood we have had our bottoms spanked, our hearts broken and our brains washed. These experiences have methodically shaped our perspectives on events and other people.

I have graduate degrees from a distinguished theological institution and years of clinical training. However my perspective is not always versatile. While driving several hundred miles from home, my car battery died over night for no apparent reason. The weather was comfortable, certainly not cold enough to drain the power from a relatively new battery. I had not left on my lights. Since these alternatives reached the boundaries of my automotive knowledge, I found myself stranded with very little expertise with which to diagnose the problem.

I called roadside assistance and waited about twenty minutes for the repair truck to rumble into the parking lot. It was everything I expected. A short slender man, appearing about thirty, in oily clothes, oily hair and a blue baseball cap slammed the truck door and approached my car. His fingernails were black with grease. His appearance suggested he had been very busy at his trade or perhaps just wearing the same overalls all week. He smelled of sweat and motor oil. His several missing or discolored teeth didn't seem to hinder his ability to chew and spit the tobacco pooling in his left cheek. I had met the quintessential car repairman! "Howdy! Got a dead bat 'try?"

The mechanic had been raised to be respectful, responding "yes sir" or "no sir" to my inquiries. I gave him a general synopsis of the problem and tried to make small talk as he connected the cables. I had to speak loudly over the powerful truck engine growling in the background, but asked if he lived nearby. He said "Yup! I grad'ated high school 'bout five miles from here." He smiled proudly as he gave me the news, revealing the apparent need for more conscientious dental care.

As we chatted, my new friend rarely matched subjects with verbs and lost the final "g" on most words requiring one. However, he had my car started in less than five minutes. He also noted a condenser had likely activated, causing the battery to drain overnight. He accurately predicted it would probably not happen again, but politely gave me his phone number in case I needed further assistance.

Some people want to be experts on everything. They enjoy listening to their own pontifications and expect others to be equally enthralled. I may have easily discounted this dirty little man with grime under his fingernails and broken grammar. I may have preferred not to share a restaurant booth with him, until he took a shower or at least washed his hands. I certainly had a broader frame of reference on just about everything…except automotive mechanics. I can read a New Testament passage from the original Greek, but this modestly educated mechanic could fix my car in minutes! On this particular issue, the little man with tobacco juice on his chin had the greater knowledge. He deserved my attention and respect.

As we expand our frame of reference, it helps to realize our personal world is not the only world. Our thoughts are not the only thoughts on a particular subject. We see and hear things and make decisions based on our unique frame of reference, but not necessarily because of fact or reality! Perceptions of what an individual says, meant to say, thought he said, and sometimes what someone *thinks they heard him say* are often colored by our unique frame of reference. Sometimes we need to see and hear the world from the other person's perspective.

Not long ago, Teri and I traveled into a popular resort village in the Appalachian Mountains. We wanted to spend a week with no phones, deadlines, bosses or meetings, where we could read, watch television, go to movies and enjoy being together.

One lazy afternoon we visited a familiar bookstore to replenish our supply of reading material. After inventorying their new titles and enjoying a latte, I approached the cashier. A pleasant young lady, probably in her twenties, welcomed me and began ringing up my purchase. She noticed the cast on my right hand, stretching to my elbow and asked if I had broken my arm. I explained I had torn a ligament and recently undergone wrist reconstruction surgery. She whispered "Ewe," shivered and continued with my purchase.

She placed the credit card slip on the counter and held it while I signed with my left hand. She remarked, "You really did that very well. How long has it been since your surgery?" I told her about three weeks and she again complimented my versatility. Assuring me of a future discount, she held another document tightly on the counter, while I entered my address and signed. She seemed genuinely impressed with how fluidly I could write and repeated how great I was doing with my left hand. I smiled, thanked her and said I had been practicing since I was two. Momentarily, the pleasant young lady seemed frozen in deep thought. Then the epiphany struck. Her face reddened as she softly said, "You're left handed aren't you?"

What the cashier perceived as challenging was something I did on a daily basis. It had not occurred I may be left handed. Her frame of reference, like that of most people, was one of right handedness. This is how we miss opportunities to resolve conflict. Sometimes the alternatives never come to mind because of our perspective is so narrowly framed.

I noticed the cashier was right handed. She probably had no friends or family who were left handed. She had no reason to suspect I was anything but right handed and wanted to express compassion for my apparent disability. She viewed the world from a right handed perspective.

She likely had no appreciation for those who live life from the other side. However, working, driving, dining, and worshipping next to you are those of us who see life from a different perspective. We were forced to do 1st grade arts and crafts with scissors designed only for right handed children. I can still remember crushing the outlines of paper pumpkins, leaves and snowmen with those horrible scissors! I had the hardest time understanding why using scissors was such a challenge, until my mother broke the unsettling news! We tie our shoes differently and try using your computer mouse left-handed.

However while recovering from wrist surgery I realized how often I needed both hands to get dressed. Have you ever tied a necktie or buttoned a shirt with only one hand? Taking a shower, washing your hair and using a towel create previously unimagined complexities. As frustrating as it may have been, wrist surgery enriched my frame of reference. I had a new perspective from which to draw new perceptions. Similar enlightenments often occur when people experience temporary loss of hearing or sight.

Our frame of reference on more volatile subjects such as race relations, abortion or gun control will also be influenced by personal experiences. Consider your perspective on the image below. Do you recognize it as a symbol of peace or violence?

If you are Jewish this symbol might be horrifying! How may your perspective be intensified if a family member had been imprisoned or killed at Auschwitz or one of the many Nazi death camps? How might your perspective change if your ancestors lived in Berlin, Moscow, London, or Warsaw? How about if they lived in Cleveland? Do you see how reactions may differ?

What if your husband, father or grandfather from Cleveland was killed during the D-Day invasion of Normandy or during the Battle of the Bulge? What if your only familiarity with this symbol was from a history book? Do you see how our emotional responses and perspectives might change, depending on our frame of reference?

For most of us, this object symbolizes all that is wrong with society. Even on the surface, it represents racism, hatred, violence, genocide, and political extremism. The passing of time, personal or ancestral experience, historical references and religious beliefs have constructed our frame of reference about this object. Right or wrong, it is our perspective and will not be easily changed.

Now, imagine you are living in Mesopotamia in about 300 BCE. Are you surprised to know the swastika is actually a cross? Until corrupted by Adolph Hitler and the Nazi Party, it served many as a symbol of good luck, life, the sun and prosperity. The swastika has been around for almost 3000 years. Originally called the gammadion cross, it is constructed with four *gammas*, the third letter in the Greek alphabet. In Scandinavian mythology, it is inscribed on Thor's hammer and appears on coins from ancient Troy. Christian churches in the first millennium were adorned with swastikas and during World War I an American military division wore it as an arm patch. While very few of us have any desire to hang a swastika in our den for good luck, it really is a matter of perspective. We do not need to accept that perspective in order to understand it as a valid alternative.

Do you recall the mental list of *red* items you made earlier? Let's pause to think about it. Look down at your slip of paper and carefully recall the items on your mental list. Now write down everything in your environment that is ...*blue*. Got'cha!

How did you do? Did you have to cheat? Understanding how frame of reference impacts interpersonal conflict is essential for effective resolution. If I spend my time looking only for red things, I may miss all the pretty blue things. If I spend my time looking for blonds, I may miss the brunettes or girls with pretty auburn hair. If I only shop for apples, I may miss the luscious oranges, mangos, pomegranates, lemons and limes. If we do not even see them or consider them, how can we understand them or give them value? If I see only the red burning emotion of anger or rage, how will I see alternatives objectively?

If Mom goes into her teenaged daughter's room and sees only clutter, how will she see the child who lives inside? If Mom only speaks of picking up shoes, throwing dirty clothes into the hamper and making the bed, she may not recognize the child's interests, unique self- expressions or need to be heard and better understood.

If I do not understand why an issue makes me angry, while having no obvious affect on anyone else, how can we resolve our differences? Jesus said, *How can you say to your brother, Let me take the speck out of your eye, when there is a log in your own eye?*

Remember, conflict resolution begins with acknowledging our limitations: self awareness. Our frame of reference is limited to what we consider appropriate, right, logical or valid. Do these parameters need broadening? Also important is realizing how our perspective is perceived by others. If everyone realizes I can only see the red objects in the room, while I consider myself visually diverse, I may be only fooling myself.

Once I acknowledge my frame of reference may be uninformed, emotional or biased, I begin to accept my limitations. I become aware of how I may be misunderstood or may misunderstand others. Eventually, I develop insights allowing me to seek areas of compatibility with others. I may not understand your red face and obvious frustration, until I look closely enough to realize you have been trying to clip out your coupon with my left-handed scissors.

THREE

FERTILE GROUND FOR CONFLICT

Interpersonal conflict tends to live up to its name. It usually involves people who are very different. Have you noticed how logic does not work for everyone? Try taping a sign in a stairwell, on a park bench, wall or a doorframe that reads, "Wet Paint. Do Not Touch." Rest assured if enough people go by, despite their twittering, cell phoning and texting somebody is bound to touch it!

Regardless of age, education, ethnicity, technological sophistication, or disciplined childhood, some people will not believe the provocative little sign applies to them. Perhaps they simply need to know if it is wet enough to allow a finger to slurve a squiggly line or write three initials. Regardless, human nature dictates that given enough time and opportunity, someone will have to know!

People make choices for very personal, often inexplicable reasons. Some people follow rules and do not touch things when told not to touch. If a recipe calls for ¼ teaspoon of vanilla extract, they search every drawer in the kitchen until they find the correct measuring utensil. Others just slop it in. Some people are naturally inquisitive and need to discover things for themselves. They bring home a container with a new DVD player, throw the instructions to the side and start assembling the assorted parts. Others read the instructions carefully, even jotting notes before they dare touch the plastic baggies filled with parts.

Some people refuse to allow logic to take them from point A to point B. Just like some choose not to believe the "Wet Paint" sign or think of it as a mere suggestion. It is from these different perspectives that interpersonal conflict stirs serious and often long lasting consequences.

God gave Adam and Eve access to a world of unimaginable splendor called the Garden of Eden. It was theirs to celebrate! But with this gift came specific instructions, *You may freely eat of every tree of the garden; but of the tree of the knowledge of good and evil you shall not eat, for in the day that you eat of it you shall die* (Gen 2:16-17). The resulting chain of events offer remarkable insights into interpersonal conflict as it continues into the 21st century.

TWO FORMS OF CONFLICT

Substantive and *Relationship* are two primary forms of interpersonal conflict. *Substantive Conflict* is usually about substance or *stuff*. It is the easiest form of conflict to recognize and resolve. It involves specific facts (2+2=4, not 5 or 6), rules, procedures or even opinions. God said in terms even an unsophisticated guy like Adam could understand, "If you eat from the Tree of Knowledge you're going to die." Could he have made himself any clearer? *Wet Paint- Do Not Touch!*

Substantive Conflict is not very complicated. "Do not eat the fruit!" You can smell the fruit, look at it, touch it, compare it to other fruit, even pick the fruit and carry it around in your basket, but don't eat it. If a reasonably well trained crime scene investigator can find traces of fruit juice on your hands, tooth marks in the fruit or your fingerprints on the tree branches, how much easier will it be for God? "Don't eat the fruit!"

Relationship Conflict is far more complicated, involving unpredictable human dynamics. It includes tricky, hard to control things like trust, communication, perceptions and forgiveness.

Imagine the scene as Adam arrived home, thinking aloud about his hard day of naming animals, *there were the octopi, hippopotami, and the dragonflies, lions and tigers and bears, Oh, my...what have you done?* As Eve stood there, fruit juice dripping from her big toothy grin and down her chin, he knew the rules had been eternally broken. Conflict was at hand!

A FAMILIAR STRUGGLE

Conflict may be intra-personal and interpersonal in the church, family, classroom, or business relationship. Eve's struggle with conscience to disobey God began as intra-personal conflict. This was not unlike Hamlet's struggle "to be or not to be." However, it became interpersonal when she gave Adam a bite. It became even more complex when Adam and Eve's eyes were opened and *they knew that they were naked* (Gen 3:7), realizing the consequences of their actions. The best of times had become the worst of times!

Eve knew it was wrong to eat the fruit. Adam knew it was wrong. Substantive conflict had occurred. They had broken the rules. But, these were God's rules! Suddenly, Adam and Eve recognized each other's weaknesses and their sin before God. Relationships were in conflict also. Making matters worse, God was sending them out of their garden sanctuary for all creation to see.

In 2009, Gov. Mark Sanford of South Carolina reportedly admitted to his wife he had been having an affair with a journalist from Argentina.[1] He admitted his actions were sinful and appeared remorseful. He and his wife, Jenny, began trying to repair their marriage. However, when he later disappeared for several days, reportedly to visit again with his Argentine lover, the conflict between Mark and Jenny became a group dynamic. The governor's staff was unable to reach him for several days. Like God walking through the garden, the local media began searching for the missing governor and for the truth.

As Gov. Sanford returned from Argentina, a newspaper reporter saw him walking through an Atlanta airport. She stopped him and asked where he had been. "What is this you have done?" rang her question from the ancient Garden of Eden. He had taken a bite of the forbidden fruit and in a matter of hours, newspaper and television reporters from local, regional and national affiliates picked up the story. Realizing his story would be in the next morning's newspaper, on June 24, 2009, Gov. Mark Sanford tearfully confessed to a national television audience. His character flaws were exposed for all to see and judge. He knew what it meant to be naked before God.

This particular conflict went beyond the governor's intra-personal struggle whether to remain faithful or to go again to Argentina. It went beyond his interpersonal marital conflict. This conflict had reached biblical proportions! Everyone who watched his televised confession or read it in the newspapers would be drawn into his conflict, struggling to decide whether to forgive or to remove him from the Garden.

Breaking the rules was substantive conflict, until it wounded the heart of his wife and four sons. Breaking the rules and being caught proved only the beginning. Time would tell if the many relationships his actions damaged would ever be healed or if he could remain in office after betraying his constituents.

The Garden of Eden story offers an interesting perspective on the two primary forms of conflict. It also offers insights into some of the many complications that cause these interpersonal conflicts to be so hard to resolve.

PERSONALITY

Personality complications are just what they imply. Adam appears to have been a simple guy. The Scriptures do not suggest he had given much thought to the Tree of Knowledge of Good and Evil or the implications of eating its fruit. The Tree of Life is also mentioned, but Adam still does not appear very curious. He does not seem to search for the meaning of life, but he must have had a creative side. God brought him creatures just to see what he would name them!

Eve appears inquisitive. She took long walks through the garden, talking with serpents and wondering what might happen if she didn't follow the rules. She seemed to be a global thinker, looking outside the box. I can imagine her peering over the garden walls or between the hedges, wondering what adventures waited just beyond her reach. Was the grass really greener out there? Little did she know she would soon find out!

Eve seems very sensual. She saw the tree was good for food and was a delight to the eyes. She seemed intuitive, curious and appreciated beauty. Clearly, Adam and Eve demonstrated very different personalities. Would these differences lead to conflict? Does it ever?

Perhaps Adam would have noticed the Tree of Knowledge of Good and Evil after he finished naming all the animals. Sometimes after watching a ballgame, guys notice the lawn needs mowing or the clogged gutters. Anyway, Adam and Eve appear very different and possibly ate the forbidden fruit for different reasons. However, as soon as the finger pointing started, their relationship suffered. When Adam complained to God about Eve giving him the fruit, I can imagine Eve murmuring, "If I told you to jump off a bridge, would you do that too?"

When personality differences are ignored, either in the office, the boardroom, the church, or at the family dinner table, interpersonal conflict gains considerable opportunity for disrupting the covenant relationship. Eventually we look around and realize we're not in the Garden anymore.

ATTITUDES

Another complication occurs when attitudes conflict. Do you know anyone who has a bad attitude? How can you miss them? What does it mean to have a bad attitude? Eve believed the Tree of Knowledge of Good and Evil was a good source of food and wisdom, so she took a bite. The eternal God of the universe, the omnipotent creator of all living creatures had said, "You shall not eat!" What made her think eating the fruit was an option?

Something in Eve's understanding of this commandment made her wonder what would happen? She was the only female in the garden. Would God really cause her to die if she ate the forbidden fruit? Surely, God loved her and his creation too much to let something like that happen. What led her to this misguided sense of entitlement? What made Eve feel invincible and beyond the reach of God? What makes any of us do such a thing?

Attitudes come in all sorts. They are not always bad, sometimes just hard to handle. Childhood influences, social injustices, racial slurs, past failures and accomplishments, acknowledgements and omissions flow through the fabric of our personality. They create attitudes affecting our interpersonal relationships, which bring heightened complexities into a conflict. What may have been only substantive conflict, "Do not eat the fruit" becomes "I will eat the fruit. I may even eat all of the fruit and there's nothing you can do about it!"

COMMUNICATION

Most of us consider ourselves good communicators, but do the people with whom we communicate consider us good communicators? Communication potentially causes any interpersonal conflict to worsen with the turn of a phrase. God said, *You may freely eat of every tree of the garden; but of the tree of the knowledge of good and evil you shall not eat, for in the day that you eat of it, you shall die* (Gen. 2: 16-17). That seemed unmistakably clear until the serpent stirred some ambiguity into the mix.

The serpent began by challenging the content of God's prohibition. Look between the lines. Imagine the serpent drawing Eve into his deceptive little world, "Do you think you may have misunderstood what God said? Did God say you couldn't eat of any trees? They're awfully pretty and have to be nourishing, with a divinely inspired, vitamin-enriched taste." Eve wasn't hooked at first. She reminded the serpent she had taken very clear notes and understood God to say, "You shall not eat of the tree which is in the midst of the garden."

I have no doubt what came next. It might have been omitted from the text, but I'm convinced the serpent's next argument suggested the Tree of Knowledge of Good and Evil was not in the geographical *midst of the garden* and possibly not the tree in question. But the specific location of the fruit was not the real issue! The serpent also challenged the intent of God's prohibition. God said they would die. The serpent said, "You will not die! It's just a scare tactic to keep you from having your eyes opened."

These games of semantics and manipulation become familiar obstructions in interpersonal conflict resolution. Good communicators say what they mean and verify what was heard.

EMOTIONS

Emotions are the most disruptive of the complications. *Then the Lord God said to the woman, "What is this you have done?"* (Gen 3:13). How many times has an incredulous mother uttered those same words to a child who has just emptied a pitcher of orange juice onto the floor, drawn crayon pictures on the Living Room wall or eaten a stick of butter? When well-known politicians announce extra-marital affairs to the news media, a collective, "What is this you have done?" is written in newspaper editorials and heard by pundits on 24-hour news shows. When you unintentionally roll your grocery cart into the fender of a nearby car or when a police officer walks to your car window, with blue lights reflecting in your mirror, the same question challenges: "What is this you have done?" The result in each case, if only fleeting, is emotional. An abrupt, ill-conceived emotional reaction may seriously complicate matters.

Relationships complicated by emotions, no matter whether from righteous indignation or because spiritual or psychological buttons have been pushed, have the greatest potential for disaster. They bring painful retaliations. Emotions are primal, seldom rational and easily get in the way. We want to hit back. They must be quickly acknowledged and effectively managed in conflict resolution. This is a critical, non-negotiable rule!

A GRACIOUS SOLUTION

The Garden of Eden story shows how complications quickly arise from a single series of events. It illustrates how conflict may have long lasting consequences and how it can be resolved graciously. The greater message in the Garden of Eden story is found not in Adam and Eve's sin, but in God's solution.

God knew the rules were broken. He also realized the paralyzing affects of Adam and Eve's fear, anxiety, guilt and shame. He would have been justified to bring death upon them in unimaginable ways. However, resolving conflict graciously is seldom about being right or justified. It is more often about realizing the value of relationships and finding a means of reconciliation. God gave Adam and Eve a second chance, only outside the garden.

In the Sermon on the Mount, Jesus compared his message with the scribes and Pharisees. While discussing the matter of bringing gifts into the temple, he said, "leave your gift there before the altar and go; first be reconciled to your brother." The Garden of Eden story asks if we who have been created in God's image will choose to look beyond ourselves to better understand and reconcile our differences with others. Will we choose to be gracious, even when we are right, justified or have the better argument or will we elect simply to win at all costs? These are the questions of conflict resolution. Not unlike Adam and Eve, we will have to work to find the answers.

FOUR

SOME IMAGES ARE MORE DIVINE THAN OTHERS

Humanity is created in God's image. Of course, some images are more divine than others. In the "The Acts of Paul and Thecla," written some time before AD 200, a man went out with his children to greet the apostle Paul as he arrived in town. The following description ensured Paul would not be missed:

> *A small man of stature, with a bald head and crooked legs,*
> *in a good state of body, with eyebrows meeting and nose*
> *somewhat hooked, full of friendliness.*

Apparently, the apostle Paul may not have been the tall, ruggedly handsome Roman intellectual your mind conjures as you read his letters. Instead, the evidence suggests he may have more likely been a short, bald, guy with one eyebrow and an engaging smile. Perhaps this is not unlike trying to imagine the appearance of a potential love interest while engaged in on-line dating.

So what does it mean to be created in God's image? Perhaps it has to do with physical appearance, such as the familiar image of God as an aged grandfather, complete with white beard and indulgent eyes. In this case, the description of St. Paul might be more representative of God's image on a bad day!

Perhaps since God is perfect, you and I who are created in his image are also expected to meet that standard. Having studied interpersonal conflict for decades, I can assure you we are not! In fact, those who insist they are perfect, simply create a little more conflict for the rest of us! So, where are we going with this?

Humanity may be created in God's image, but we come in all shapes and sizes. We are introverted, extroverted, thoughtful, emotional, structured, methodical and spontaneous. We are dog-people and cat-people. Some of us are apparently from Mars and some from Venus.

One of my quiet pleasures is to observe the subtle or sometimes overt idiosyncrasies, indulgences and rituals found in church pews, airplanes, subway trains, congested traffic and in office meetings. However, I can think of no better cultural Petrie dish of human behavior than New York City during the holidays.

Teri and I were married on Staten Island and return to New York City each year for our anniversary on December twenty-eighth. If you have ever experienced New York just after Christmas, but right before the Rockin' New Year's Eve, you understand what a cultural phenomenon it can be. The crowds are a mass of padded elbows, gloved fingers and frosted breath! Multi-ethnic pilgrims bundled in heavy coats and scarves, shivering in the icy wind, move in unison along the congested sidewalks.

The fluid movement of the masses along Broadway and 7th Avenue often follows the rules of traveling the American highways. Thousands walking uptown travel along the right side of the sidewalk. Folks going downtown, travel along the left. Of course, a frustrated few will race around in the street to beat the crowd to the next corner.

The slow moving crowd obediently stops for the flashing red pedestrian lights on each corner, making way for police cars, limousines and racing yellow cabs. Tourists often stand amused and sometimes horrified by the reckless abandon with which the New York cabbies transport their fares across the crowded city.

Occasionally a freethinking maverick interrupts the orderly progression to aim a digital camera, read a subway map or to admire the flashing lights creating the phenomenon known as Times Square. Conventional wisdom says the easiest way to spot a tourist in New York City is to wait long enough for him to stop and gaze upward in jaw-dropping amazement at the skyscrapers. Collisions and curses from the locals soon follow.

Our favorite place to stay is the Edison Hotel. It is not one of those ritzy, uptown hotels, famous for having its facade in the movies. Nor was it built by an eccentric entrepreneur, with notoriously bad hair. It is just a quiet, older hotel nestled along 48th Street between 8th Avenue and Broadway, in the heart of the Theater District. It is comfortable and not horribly expensive, as New York hotel rates go. Its front door is located only a block away from Times Square.

Early one morning, Teri and I were riding the hotel elevator to the lobby. Our immediate goal was to slip over to a nearby coffee shop for some desperately needed caffeine and then down to the 42nd St subway station. From there we would make our way to the unique shopping venues of Canal Street and SoHo.

As the elevator stopped on the Eighth Floor, a well-dressed, middle-aged man entered. He was warmly dressed for the blustery weather in a heavy black overcoat, hat and gloves. He pulled a large suitcase on rollers and carried a black garment bag across his arm. He smiled, nodded and offered a very pleasant "Good Morning." He had to be in sales or maybe just a morning person, because he seemed a little too chipper for that time of day! Then, for no apparent reason, he clumsily draped his garment bag across his other arm, said, "Pardon me" and reached in front of me to press the already illuminated "L" button. What was he thinking?

We were on our way to the Lobby! How could you tell? Well, we had already pressed the "Lobby" button on the panel, it was brightly lit and we were going *down*. I am sure the arrow above the elevator door indicated we were going that direction just before it opened! So why did he find the need to inconvenience himself, switching his garment bag from one arm to the other, to re-press an already illuminated button? What about this process did he not understand?

As I thought about this curiosity, we stopped on the Fourth Floor. A young couple, probably in their twenties stepped into the elevator. The young woman held the hand of their little boy who was bundled in his snowsuit, no doubt ready for a wintery Times Square adventure. She carried a large purse and a bag of snacks across her other arm. The young man was fidgeting with his camera case, with one arm in his coat sleeve. He reached across the executive and me with his other arm to press the illuminated "L" button. Now, I had to pause for a brief moment to ask myself calmly why he did such a thing. IT WAS ALREADY LIT!

I began wondering about this image of God thing. If God entered my elevator while on the way to the hotel lobby and saw I had pressed the "L" button, I am convinced he would not press it again. He would trust me to get us there! Maybe after Adam took a bite of the fruit given to him by his companion, trust was something we lost in the Garden of Eden. Realistically, if we cannot trust a little light in an elevator, how we trust a God we cannot see, hear, smell or touch? How can we believe when Jesus says, "I will be with you always?" How will we trust our teenaged son when he says, "I didn't have anything to drink"?

Not long ago, I pulled into a well-known fast food restaurant during the heart of lunchtime. The drive-through line was backed into the street. I could see patrons reading newspapers, texting, talking on cell phones, waiting for their turn at the magical microphone that would soon bring nourishment. I decided to go inside. Surely, the line had to be quicker and I could save a few gallons of gas!

Several teenagers wearing the prescribed paper hats and crisp, although probably embarrassing uniforms were taking orders from a mass of patrons, most of whom had clearly not eaten in weeks! Starving customers formed three closely packed serving lines, extending from the cash registers to the condiment bar and beyond. The nearest line made a nasty curve towards the front door! I was not sure this was a good idea and gave serious thought to leaving. Then, I noticed something curious. While I had seen only three heavily populated serving lines, there were four!

I made my way around the condiment bar, squeezed past a few closely positioned tables and excused myself past several patrons carrying trays loaded with enough food for several day's journey into the wilderness. I approached the counter, noticing only one lady in the serving line. For a moment, I thought she was waiting to pick up her order or asking for a drink refill. As she left, no one stepped to the counter. The young man in his neat paper hat and broad smile welcomed me. He took my order, while everyone else waited in the other lines. He clearly recognized someone created in God's image.

I do not understand why perilously hungry people, in three crowded lines, remained in their respective lines, while a perfectly capable young man was willing to take their order. Could these people also be created in God's image? Maybe this explains why we are called to remember it was the Tree of Knowledge *of Good and Evil*, not just the Tree of Knowledge. These folks may have inherited a divine discernment of good and evil, but they were having a lot of trouble with good old common sense!

Perhaps being created in God's image says less about perfection or God's physical characteristics than about his nature as The Creator! Maybe that is why, like no other animal, humans create things like poetry, music and art. We also have the unique ability to cultivate reason and develop abstract thought.

After tasting the fruit of the Tree of Knowledge, man became like God, knowing good and evil. Then, his eye suddenly focused on the Tree of Life and immortality. However, read the Scripture carefully. It says man has *become like* God. It does not say man *has become God*. A considerable difference is found in these two statements.

As Adam and Eve became *like* God, they gained the capacity to discern between good and evil. However, they were not gods. The difference suggests our actions will not always bring godly results. For the first time, Adam and Eve experienced nakedness, but they had been naked all along. Suddenly they understood what it meant to be exposed in front of God and others. As they walked from their precious Garden and saw it locked by the hand of God, they experienced and understood new concepts such as embarrassment, guilt, shame, fear, loss and grief. These concepts would follow their ancestors into the 21st century and beyond.

As Adam and Eve understood their nakedness, they also realized God had clothed them. Apparently, it was in God's nature to bring comfort and to sustain his creation, even when it disappointed him, failed to live up to his standards or created unnecessary conflict.

Human nature is a conundrum. We are a mystery. We are a perplexing bunch! People will press elevator buttons that have already been pressed. We will wait in long lines to be served, while empty lines are nearby. We will do stupid things, illogical things and silly things. We will do things for the sake of sentiment or meanness or love.

Some people will carelessly talk on cell phones while driving. They will send text messages in movie theaters and bring too many items to the *Ten Items or Less* line. They will be annoying, insulting, obnoxious and hurtful. They will also be loving, tender, caring and thoughtful. They will laugh inappropriately and cry for no reason. They will be impatient, indulgent and sometimes moronic! They will lie, cheat, steal and think only of themselves. People will be people ... and we will want to drive them as far out of our Garden as possible!

However, to be created in God's image means we are capable of discerning good from evil. We are capable of creating alternatives when no viable alternatives or solutions seem possible. We are capable of looking beyond our own self-interests. We are capable of recognizing and clothing nakedness. Perhaps this is what Jesus meant when he said to love the Lord thy God with all thy heart and love thy neighbor as you love yourself. This becomes very important when trying to resolve interpersonal conflict.

Because human beings are so unique and often profoundly annoying to each other, conflict is usually unavoidable. It is not personal, just inevitable! Interpersonal conflict is a part of the human equation, just like paying taxes and dying. The better we equip ourselves to recognize and accept these truths, the more effective we will be in handling it. As we become more willing to accept, appreciate and work within our differences, the more effectively we will cope with traffic jams, restaurant lines, crowded department stores, the office, and even telemarketers.

A critical component in resolving inter-personal conflict is realizing we are all created in God's image. By learning to appreciate and cultivate that gift, we also develop skills to understand and creatively control a special part of the Garden that Adam and Eve failed to control: *ourselves!*

It may be enlightening to understand why the New York businessman or young father inconvenienced himself to press an already lit elevator button. It may be an interesting psychological study to assess why people stand in one line, while opportunities are waiting in another. However, it may be more personally significant for me to understand why I care. Self-awareness can be a tricky thing!

FIVE

TOAST SWEAT AND OTHER ANNOYANCES

It is an unsettling fact. With all of our faults and idiosyncrasies, conflict is poised at every turn. The human equation is the variable within each interpersonal conflict that cannot be predicted with very much precision. For that reason, you never can tell how things may turn out.

Bill and Kathy had been married only about eighteen months, but they were struggling to stay together. They sat quietly side by side, almost touching, but separated all the same. An obvious tension bathed the room. Kathy's eyes focused on her hands. She twisted her wedding rings around her finger, seemingly contemplating whether to take them off or wear them a little longer. Bill seemed similarly uncomfortable as his eyes surveyed the shelves of books around my office. Both appeared uncertain who should cast the first stone.

Finally, Kathy said, "I just can't take it anymore. He's a slob!" Her words broke the silence only momentarily. He looked down at his shoes, almost as if to see if he had tracked mud into my office. She stared at me, presumably waiting to see on which side of their self imposed fence I would fall. Instead, I asked for clarification. After several minutes, I realized their problem came down to *Toast Sweat*.

Toast sweat is an unusual phenomenon occurring when a fresh hot piece of toast is left on the kitchen counter. After a few minutes, when you pick up the toast, a residual condensation has formed on the counter: *Toast Sweat*.

After several more conversations, Kathy began to realize she loved Bill very much. She also realized she would never fashion him into the perfect husband. As much as she complained, he still left his socks on the floor, tracked mud through the house, left the his pants on the back of the chair, left the toilet seat up, dishes on the kitchen counter after his *midnight* snack and toast sweat on the counter. How could she live with such a slob?

Fortunately, Kathy soon realized removing *toast sweat* and other annoyances from her world were not as important as keeping Bill in it. Conversely, it became easier for her to remember the many reasons she married him. The less she judged and criticized, the less tension they felt in their relationship. As their communication transitioned from complaining and sarcasm to sincerity and honesty, they began to understand each other better. Bill's forgetfulness curiously began to improve, not because he wanted to avoid a confrontation, but because he wanted to please his wife. Kathy knew she wanted to spend the rest of her life in Bill's arms. Some things are more important than toast sweat!

Realistically, if you date someone long enough, live or work with someone, or just spend a lot of time around other people, eventually irritations will surface. We can't help it! If we are careful not to leave our dirty dishes on the kitchen counter, we may just as easily be criticized for being a clean freak. Television commercials at any time of day remind us we have body odor, bad breath, split ends, blemishes and the wrong color or thinning hair. We are tense, irritable and sometimes a little gassy. We can't be as perfect as other people need or expect us to be.

Accidents happen, even to careful people. Errors in judgment happen, even to thoughtful discerning people. Appointments are missed, milk is spilled, dishes are broken and toast sweat happens! Such is life! C'est la vie! We will find ourselves in fewer conflicts as soon as we begin to accept that certainty.

Conversely, the only part of a conflict I know I can control is *ME*. If I make a concerted effort, I can control my thoughts, words and behavior. This helps me control the outcome. It also helps lessen everyday stress and improves my capacity to resolve conflict. I may not be able to control what you think or say or how you say it, but I can control my response. That is a tremendous first step and where all conflict resolution should begin!

Tina is a highly educated analyst for a large company. She takes her job seriously and her work is meticulous. She takes pride in being organized, prepared and highly professional in every meeting. She expects perfection from herself and invests a great deal of attention to detail. She needs structure, timelines and specific instructions.

Barbie is her supervisor. She is responsible for a critical company component and is frequently expected to make presentations to the senior management. She supervises a team of seven, but with the finesse of a rodeo clown. She is often unprepared for staff meetings, but does not realize it until the meeting has begun. She takes personal calls while the team discusses key strategies and loses important documents, often expecting Tina or others to reconstruct them. She has over two-hundred unread emails at any given time and finds her automated calendar much too complicated.

Barbie and Tina frequently clash during important staff meetings. Barbie often has no idea what a project needs beyond its basic scope and Tina needs specifics! As Tina becomes increasingly frustrated, she asks for more and more detail. Barbie has none and feels threatened by Tina's constant interruptions.

Since Barbie is her boss, Tina struggles to find ways of avoiding these unproductive confrontations. She jots shopping lists on her pad, usually intended for annotating important details. She reminds herself, "This is my job and today I'm being paid to listen while Barbie reads this five-page document to us." She and an equally frustrated colleague make faces or smirk while Barbie fumbles through a stack of papers looking for a report everyone except her has read. Tina also self medicates with anti-anxiety medication to calm herself when the frustrations reach excruciating levels.

Barbie is middle-aged, only a few years from retirement and will not likely change her behavior. In every meeting, Tina may pelt her with enough questions to make her feel insecure, incompetent, or grossly unprepared. Tina may constantly insist on expressing her frustrations over Barbie's lack of organization, indecisiveness or unbridled spontaneity. However, one day Barbie will find the "Start" button on her computer. It may take several hours, but she will eventually find the necessary file and prepare Tina's annual performance evaluation. Barbie will get revenge!

Tina's only productive solution, beyond trying to express her concerns to Barbie, between personal phone calls, is to realize the source of her frustration is Barbie's behavior: not Barbie. There is a difference!

Kathy eventually realized she loved Bill very much. It was his annoying behavior she did not like. Consequently, life with Bill and all of his irritations was better than life without him.

Tina's decision will be similar. She needs to decide if she has made the correct career choice. If she decides she has a good job, with a good company, she will have to acknowledge it will likely never be the perfect job. Barbie will never be the perfect boss, but it is her behavior that creates most of the conflict. If Tina decides to keep her job, it becomes important for her to learn to control her responses to Barbie's behavior, while accepting her as an imperfect, distracted, often ill-prepared individual. That leads her to a simple strategy.

Barbie's behavior will become symbolic *toast sweat*. Every time Tina goes into a meeting, she will imagine herself finding toast sweat on the kitchen counter. This gives her choices. She can get mad, throw things, complain, wipe it up, walk away or choose to cook an enjoyable breakfast despite the annoyance. She is free to react emotionally and unproductively, further antagonizing Barbie, or respond professionally.

Tina will only have control over one person during those annoying meetings: *herself.* Expecting Barbie to be different or *new and improved* in the next meeting is an effort in futility. Tina's new strategy will give her permission to be only as productive during the next meeting as circumstances will allow. She will control only what she can effectively control. She will focus on behavior and not the person. This strategy works with any unavoidable annoyance. The point is to give yourself permission to focus on the big picture. This can be your marriage, family, job, project, or sanity.

Such is life. Since the Garden of Eden, it will never be perfect again. Jobs will never be perfect. People will never be perfect. Tina cannot re-create Barbie into her own image. She will have to accept her as part of the imperfect world in which she has chosen to reside. How she chooses to reconcile herself to Barbie's behavior and work on improving their relationship are important pieces in the interpersonal conflict resolution puzzle. Sometimes life's greatest accomplishment is to be at peace with ourselves.

SIX

THOU SHALT NOT
SUBSTANTIVE CONFLICT

"You should have gone between Sunday school and Worship." "I didn't have to go then." "Well, you can't go now. You'll just have to wait." Most parents with small children have experienced this intense, although whispered exchange at least once. Parents set rules intended to teach children social skills and proper etiquette. Children pay those rules very little attention until they bring inconvenient or unexpected consequences. This is the nature of substantive conflict.

Substantive conflict appeared in Scripture as early as the Garden of Eden. God told Adam and Eve not to eat from the Tree of Knowledge of Good and Evil. However, after only a few suggestive phrases from the serpent, they were crunching away!

Substantive Conflict is about facts or their interpretation, ideas, opinions or procedures. Drivers of all ages and with various levels of experience recognize a red octagonal, usually found at corners or an intersection is a Stop sign. It literally means *stop your vehicle!* It is not a suggestion, proposal, point of debate or an alternative. It gives one instruction: STOP. Anything other than stopping is in conflict. The police officer writing your ticket will be able to cite the specific municipal or state code of law to confirm this fact.

Of course, the actual conflict usually occurs with interpretation. How long of a pause constitutes a stop? I recall an older, more experienced driver who was convinced the highway department actually sanctioned the *rolling stop*. This is the process by which impatient drivers slowly approach a stop sign, but feel justified to keep the flow of traffic moving if the coast is clear.

Substantive conflict in its simplest form is illustrated as 2+2=5. No combination of two items plus another two items can result in a total other than four items. The resolution of the conflict is as simple as placing two items on a table, then adding two more items and counting them: one- two- three- four: not five!

Substantive conflict occurs when you are driving through your neighborhood at forty-five miles per hour while passing a sign that reads: 35 MPH. You are in substantive conflict with the legal authorities and community representatives who established the prescribed speed limit.

Suppose you approach a storefront with the sign "Business Hours from 9:00am to 9:00pm." As a product of the retail sales industry, I know intimately the question that charges through the mind of every potential customer, "What if I get inside by 9:00pm, do they not still have to serve me?" Your perspective is in substantive conflict with every store employee who planned to leave work on time.

Signs such as *Do Not Enter, Do Not Touch* or *Keep off the Grass* tend to invite substantive conflict. Even a statement such as *"Your curfew is 11:30pm"* lends itself to interpretation. Does Dad mean in the driveway, on the front porch making out or in the house?

Does the commandment *Thou Shalt Not Kill* refer only to killing people or also animals? How does it apply if my family and I are threatened with bodily harm? How does it apply during wartime or to capital punishment? After all, the Bible also sanctions *an eye for an eye*! If it applies to animals, does it preclude killing for the sake of food or if the animal is rabid? At first glance, it seemed so simple.

The key to understanding and determining the amount of energy needed to resolve substantive conflict is considering the consequences. Are meticulously accurate mathematical calculations essential to save the world from an approaching rogue comet from outer space? If the answer is "Yes," a considerable investment is immediately required. If a definitive answer is not needed for the next two hundred years, the conflict requires less intensity.

Another consequence to consider is whether the substantive conflict may eventually lead to adversity within an important relationship. Teri and I love to go to movies. It is our escape from life's unavoidable conflicts. We tend to enjoy the same types of movies, but sometimes need to compromise. I will go to "chick flicks" and occasionally enjoy them. She likes action and adventure movies, but we do not always see eye to eye on the level of acceptable violence and mayhem. However while we usually accommodate each other's preferences without much debate, our level of enjoyment is not always the same. We usually spend the drive home debating the esoteric details, directorial merits or redeeming social value of the movie. She has viewed the movie from her unique perspective and I have viewed it from mine.

The teenager vampire romance movie *Twilight* (Summit Entertainment, 2008) is a great example. It tells the story of a teenage girl who falls in love with a vampire, risking her future in the normal world of her friends and possibly her eternal soul. Teri found the novel by Stephanie Meyer and the subject matter provocative. She also enjoyed reading the weekly tabloids about the theatrics, the teen frenzy and the attractive stars. I have always enjoyed a good vampire movie, but this was slightly less credible than the Bella Lugosi classics I knew as a child. The scene where a host of twenty-something vampire hunks played baseball in a vacant lot on the pinnacle of a blood curdling free for all was a little more than I could bear, without a snicker.

Teri and I have differing opinions about the movie. We can see each other's different perspective without agreeing, but only substantive conflict exists. No emotion influences the discussion, beyond the passion in expressing our differing opinions. We can agree to disagree, but our conflict remains substantive. It has no meaningful negative impact on our relationship.

Through the last few years, I have enjoyed learning to cook. I understand words like roux (a mixture of flour and butter or other fat to thicken sauces), mirepoix (a French term for combining chopped onions, celery and carrots) and chiffonade (finely shredding herbs such as basil). I can prepare a cheese sauce and bake a cheesecake from scratch.

I find it flattering when someone compliments my culinary creations, but my skills are not refined to the point of taking offense if something needs improvement. I am thrilled when my mother asks for my recipe or compliments a dish. If she offers constructive criticism, I respect and appreciate her opinion. Only substantive conflict has occurred, with no adverse consequences.

On the other hand, if I appeared in Chef Julia Child's kitchen, blabbering criticisms about her most prized recipes, I doubt the circumstances would remain substantive. She likely would be polite and tolerant for only a short time. Then, if I continued, I might be shown the door with an iron skillet passing overhead.

I have debated with colleagues for hours over the meaning of Genesis Chapter One. Are the days interpreted as 24-hour days or is it possible they represent ions of time? Does the chapter mean something more theological than historical or scientific? The discussion often became passionate, but never threatened our relationship. The conflict focused only on the substance of the argument. It was not personal!

Substantive Conflict is the easiest conflict to resolve because it generally involves no aggressive emotion or personality clashes. It is simple and straightforward. Thou shalt or thou shalt not. It is not complex or disruptive until we begin to interpret, translate, manipulate or personalize the issue. This may cause it to transform into something very conflicting.

SEVEN

IF YOU HAD BEEN HERE!
RELATIONSHIP CONFLICT

"Katie doesn't do her share of the work!" Several disgruntled employees issued this complaint about a new co-worker in their small office. Complaints included too many personal phone calls, surfing the internet and taking too much time for breaks. Every time Bud, their supervisor, slipped inconspicuously through the work area, Katie seemed focused on her duties. He could not find any substance to the complaints, yet they continued almost every day.

Finally, Bud decided the constant bickering had to stop! He would prove Katie did her share of the work. He developed a new workflow, intended to provide clear proof of everyone's productivity. If he could track everyone's work objectively and demonstrate factual evidence, the conflict would be … I stopped him as he masterfully detailed the new and improved workflow. I said, "Bud, you can throw all sorts of facts and figures at these people. You can compile six months of data and prove beyond any doubt that everyone has the same level of productivity and the next day they will complain about the color of her shoes. This is not about productivity, facts or phone calls. They don't like her! You can't fix this with a spreadsheet!"

This experienced supervisor knew his office had conflict. He simply misunderstood it. Generally, substantive conflict can be resolved with the presentation of facts, figures and logic. This conflict centered on relationships within the team of workers. Until Bud addressed their dislike for Katie or she did something to change their minds, the complaints would continue.

Husbands and wives, parents and children, even co-workers disagree all the time. Teri and I can see the same movie and disagree over its merits. That does not mean our relationship is in conflict. Two colleagues may disagree over the scope of a project and prefer opposite strategies. That does not mean they are in relationship conflict…yet.

A certain man named Lazarus became very sick. He lived in the town of Bethany with his sisters Mary and Martha (John 11:1-44). The sisters sent word to Jesus that they desperately needed him, but he seemed distracted with more pressing matters. He dawdled another two days. He never seemed to get in a hurry. By the time he got to town, Lazarus had been buried four days. It was not a pretty picture.

As Jesus approached, Martha went up the road to greet him. She was polite, but it is my guess, none too pleased. She had certainly given Jesus ample notice. Why had he taken so long? Martha said, "Lord, if you had been here, my brother would not have died." Feel the passion in that statement. Her brother had died, not because of his serious illness or a lack of medical treatment, but because Jesus had taken too long! That kind of statement can put a lot of strain on a relationship.

Jesus apparently had a close relationship with this family. He had visited in their home. Mary had anointed his feet with oil and Martha served him dinner. Jesus called Lazarus his friend. He loved all three. He also knew Lazarus was deathly ill. Why had he delayed?

Later, Mary also went out to see Jesus. She looked at him with tear- stained eyes and a shattered heart, also saying, "If you had been here, my brother would not have died." Fortunately, Jesus' relationship with Mary, Martha and Lazarus included a deep and abiding trust. Even after indicting Jesus for passively contributing to her brother's death, Martha said, "And even now I know that whatever you ask from God, (he) will give you." When he saw Mary's tears, Jesus became deeply troubled that his delay had possibly inflicted so much heartache. Surely, they understood his delay was not intended to cause them grief. Still, Jesus wept.

Mary, Martha and Jesus stood at the gaping mouth of the tomb and prayed. Mary and Martha were heartbroken, but never lost their trust in Jesus. Jesus never lost his trust in God! The bonds of trust between Jesus, Mary, Martha and Lazarus and their trust in God to find a solution beyond human imagination would soon take away the acrid smell of death.

Relationships die too. They die for a number of reasons. People are said to grow apart, grow tired or too familiar. However, a key ingredient in the death of significant relationships is a loss of trust.

Relationships always have at least some minor level of trust. Think about it. Driving down the street and through an intersection requires some degree of *trust* in the other drivers to obey the traffic laws. If you go into a restaurant in Charleston, South Carolina and order their famous shrimp n' grits, you trust the chef not to put something weird or unseemly in your grits. At home, in the office, at church, this level of trust grows little by little. Each new conversation or interaction builds a new layer or corrupts an old one.

Remember your last encounter with a telemarketer. The phone rings just as you finish dinner. Reaching for the phone, your glance at the caller-ID indicates you have an "out of area" call or some other designation implying you better not pick up! Not thinking quickly enough, you answer. The caller's first few phrases are intended to settle you and begin building a rapport (trust) so you will buy their product or give them money. Telemarketing agents realize they are interrupting. They understand you do not want to talk to them. These are not trade secrets. They intentionally begin selling trust before anything else.

If you call a customer service representative to address a late charge, a certain level of trust is also needed. You want her to trust you when you say the bill arrived too late to get the check in the mail on time. You carefully select words and the proper tone to communicate you are very trustworthy. You also trust the customer service representative to be fair, objective and flexible with company policy, because you believe it is the right thing to do.

As the conversation leads you to conclude the customer service representative is not objective, fair or flexible, your trust diminishes. By the time she says "Pay up," there is very little trust left. However, symptoms of a troubled relationship are sure to linger.

You will remember that call! You may forget the customer service representative's name or voice, but you will definitely remember her response. Your relationship with her has suddenly influenced your relationship with the company for whom she works. By treating you so harshly, she fueled the perception that the company management is equally harsh and unsympathetic. You may think twice before making new purchases from this company or recommending it to a friend. This relationship is in conflict. Your perception may be incorrect, but most perceptions are considered true until proven otherwise.

An individual who is asked to trust, wonders, "Are you as good as your word?" or "If I give you an important part of myself, will you take care of it?" When trust is diminished, taken for granted, damaged or destroyed, it takes more than an apology, roses or pat on the back to put the pieces together again. Once conflict breaks the bond of trust, the process of reconciliation takes time and perseverance. Trust must be rebuilt, optimally from a solid foundation, but it will take self-awareness, self-control and considerable motivation.

It is important to realize trust is diminished incrementally during relationship conflict. The greater the offense, the greater the damage. If the original level of trust in the relationship provided a strong foundation, resolving the conflict and restoring trust will be less complicated. However, once trust is severely broken, the rebuilding process cannot begin until the two parties are willing to face each other honestly. The violation must be acknowledged and brought into the open. Until then, it is the elephant in the room. Martha and Mary laid their cards on the table, "If you had been here, my brother would not have died." It could not have been said with more clarity or pathos. Yet, Jesus was not offended.

Feelings of anger, bitterness, resentment, fear or violation may not be reasonable or even deserved, but often become entwined in conflict. It is important to discuss these emotions before addressing any other issues. Many things such as age, gender, attitude, communication and perspective will complicate conflict, but none as much as emotions.

SENSITIVITY OVERLOAD AND EMOTIONAL BURN OUT

Qualities such as empathy, compassion, patience and understanding are important when resolving interpersonal differences. Although, it is difficult to demonstrate these qualities if you are too tired to care! As an Intensive Care chaplain in a metropolitan trauma center hospital, I saw life altering crises daily. A woman brought into Intensive Care to die with congestive heart failure, a young man with brain injuries from a car accident or a gunshot victim was part of a normal day. I was assigned to care for patients and their families in three units: General, Neo-Natal and Neurological-Intensive care. The hospital had many professional chaplains and several local ministers who served as part-time chaplains. Still the need for ministry was overwhelming. Each night the faces changed but the intensity seldom eased below a simmer.

One night I sat with a tearful young mother in the Neo-Natal Unit, while we waited for her child to die. Another night I sat with several anxious family members in a congested consultation room while the physician told them their loved one had died.

For those who care for individuals in crisis, such as ministers, health care and social service workers, sensitivity overload is a complication that can overpower relationships. As you invest emotions, time and energy into caring for others, you deplete energy from your own reservoir. Gradually, you seem to lose patience with the slightest mistakes. You do not have time to listen as a friend tries to confide. Eventually, you do not have anything left to give. Sometimes even prayers become repetitious and void of passion. Resolving relationship conflict becomes very difficult. Emotional burnout has occurred.

This is also true for stay at home or working moms, who receive little support with cooking, cleaning, errands, grocery shopping, and refereeing small children. Eventually physical fatigue and emotional exhaustion cause patience to erode. Sometimes, the importance of conversation and intimacy becomes secondary to a long nap!

It is important to recognize when emotional burnout occurs. It also helps to have someone you trust who can pick up on your behavioral changes. Acknowledging overload and taking time to rest are essential. Sensitivity overload indicates your system needs to be recharged. You cannot fix everyone. You cannot be as perfect, organized or even as effective as you need to be every day. No one can! It is important to put sensitively overload in perspective. Recognize its impact on your spiritual, psychological and physical health and insist on time to heal.

Having the skills and tools to resolve conflict is of little value, if you no longer have the energy to care!

SUMMARY

Relationships are a valuable commodity! We need them to survive. They provide happiness, comfort, strength, and purpose. They represent the people we cherish: our parents, our children, our spouse, our grandparents, aunts and uncles. They include our fishing, golfing and shopping buddies, our co-workers, prayer pals and pen pals. They include the voice on the telephone trying to upgrade my telephone service and the familiar face in the picture on my dresser. Relationships create our most precious memories and stir our strongest emotions. Obviously, some are more meaningful than others. I will invest far less energy in a conflict with a telemarketer than with my spouse or daughter. Nevertheless, when conflict strikes at the heart of our relationships, especially the important ones, the reaction can be intense! The consequences may be severe or long lasting.

When the apostle Paul said, "Do not let the sun go down on your anger," he asserted the importance of relationships. Relationship conflicts may not be resolved in a day, a week or more, but they deserve our priority. They demand our attentiveness, our energy and our willingness to look beyond our own perspective for healing and reconciliation.

EIGHT

AS SIMPLE AS A-B-C

You do not have to be a rocket scientist or clinical psychologist to recognize conflict. Most of us detect it with relative ease. This is not to imply we will do anything about it! Actually, some people invest an inordinate amount of time, energy and available resources to avoid conflict! Others live under the misguided and sometimes catastrophic notion if they ignore conflict long enough, it will mystically go away. However instead of going away, it often magnifies into something unintended and very destructive.

Just because you have slammed the door, hung up the phone, sent the last text message, left the room or declared the discussion over, rarely means conflict is resolved. It usually means conflict is deferred until another day. It does not go away just because you are tired of arguing and ready to go to bed. It also tends to be a process, consisting of sequential events and behavior. Sometimes this process creates a ripple effect, reaching any number of previously uninvolved and possibly disinterested participants.

Conflict as a concept is not hard to understand. The resolution is what gets so tricky! Think of conflict as A-B-C: *Action, Behavior and Consequence.* This process is not unlike a baseball game. Imagine the batter going through his customary ritual of tightening his batting gloves, digging in the batter's box for leverage and spitting. The pitcher considers the catcher's signal and they agree on the pitch selection. Finally, the pitcher winds and throws the ball: The *Action* occurs.

51

During the instance it takes the baseball to leave the pitcher's hand and arrive at home plate, the batter constructs a *Belief*. He believes the pitch is hittable or not. This belief leads to a *Behavior*. The batter will swing at the ball or let it pass to the catcher.

Once the belief and behavior occur, the *Consequence* quickly follows. If the batter chooses not to swing, the umpire will call the pitch a ball or a strike. This may have the consequences of striking out the batter or walking him, allowing him to go to First Base. If he swings and misses, he may be more cautious with the next pitch. If the batter swings and hits the ball, another series of events occur. The hit baseball will have consequences. Of course, the ultimate result of this process in baseball is winning and losing, not reconciliation and harmony.

ACTION

Conflict begins with an *Action*, such as the thrown baseball. A more technical term is antecedent, which simply means something that gets everything rolling. This action may be an event, such your girlfriend saying you need some time apart or finding a sexually explicit text message on your teenager's cell phone.

The Action may also be a statement of fact, such as Abraham Lincoln was our 15th president or the square root of 144 is 14 or a tomato is a vegetable. It may also express an opinion, such as George W. Bush was one of America's best presidents, BMW makes excellent cars or the best color to paint the bedroom is blue. It may even be a thought, "If I ask her to the dance, she'll laugh at me" or "My child is smarter than yours" or "Those people are lazy and just want to get government handouts." None of these Actions has yet caused conflict, but they provide very fertile ground in which it can develop. After all, Abraham Lincoln was our *sixteenth* president; the square root of 144 is not 14 and you can decide for yourself about George W. Bush or BMW.

BELIEF AND BEHAVIOR

The second stage reflects a response or reaction to the action. This stage involves a *Belief* about the Action and a *Behavior*. Our beliefs are very important to us. They come from our values and our general understanding of life. If I believe the teachings of Jesus should guide me in my interpersonal relationships, my beliefs and behavior during conflict will tend to reflect those teachings. If I believe people are basically bad and self-serving, that will equally influence my actions.

These beliefs are often influenced by many different complications, which may have a considerable impact on the resulting behavior and consequences. These complications include:

Attitudes	*Gender*	*Ethnicity*	*Personality*
Communication	*Hidden Agendas*	*Emotions*	*Insecurities*
Competitiveness	*Age*	*Perceived Personal Territory*	

Have you ever noticed how two people can live in the same house, work in the same office, watch the same movie, attend the same Sunday school class or hear the same instructions and have completely different, sometimes opposing perspectives? The national healthcare debate in 2010 serves as a great example of how people can read the same information and come to opposite perspectives. Resolving this type of conflict can be exhausting, even depressing, because so many differing opinions, motivations and emotions complicate the picture.

When I see a grocery cart roll into my new car fender, my immediate reaction may be emotional! Following the whispered expletive, I scan the direction from which it came with military precision. When I see the red-faced little boy, I have a decision to make. What do I believe happened? Do I believe he pushed it too hard, missing the cart return rack, sending it into my car? Do I believe he shot the cart across the parking lot without considering where it might go or what it might hit? Do I believe he aimed for my car?

I will make this decision based on observations. What are the boy's mannerisms? Does he appear anxious or embarrassed? Does he have an incriminating smirk? Is he trying to hide or run? Is he frozen in fear and disbelief? I may also consider how fast the grocery cart was traveling when it struck my car. Was the contact similar to that of a cruise missile striking downtown Baghdad or a slight ding? This may sound complicated, but we consider these things in a matter of seconds.

On the other hand, I may have a jolt of emotion and react inappropriately! I may angrily run to the little boy and pour expletives all over his little soul, informing his parent the bill is forthcoming! However, this is not a response intended to resolve conflict. This reaction is intended to vent my emotions and get even!

If I believe the cart struck my car by accident, I may still be angry and want to confront the little urchin. Anger would not be an unexpected emotion, but if I believe the incident was accidental, I may focus on determining the amount of damage. I may give the boy an opportunity to apologize. If I believe the damage warranted repair, I could speak with his parent. My belief is critical to my response.

If I believe I should treat others as I expect to be treated, I may respond differently than if I believe *an eye for an eye*. My belief in either instance, contributes to my behavior. It causes me to react emotionally and irresponsibly or respond with controlled emotion and appropriate behavior.

Opinions are a little more troublesome. They tend to cross wires with our value system. A statement such as "George W. Bush was one of our best presidents" may bring sharp affirmations or grumbling and disagreement. Any opinion that begins "Those people" has the potential to cause a surge of emotion! Strong beliefs lead to strong behaviors. Strong behaviors lead to strong consequences.

CONSEQUENCES

Consequences provide a lasting, sometimes unpleasant, impression of our beliefs and behavior. An Action leads to a Belief and subsequent Behavior, which results in some sort of Consequence: *A-B-C.*

When the little boy and his grocery cart dinged my car, my harsh, inappropriate behavior might have a reciprocal affect. My aggressive behavior may cause his parent to perceive a threat, resulting in a call to the police or aggression towards me. In this case, the conflict actually builds upon itself. If my belief caused me to respond calmly and appropriately, the resulting consequence may bring an apology and the phone number of his insurance company.

This ABC process may be illustrated in the following sequences of events:

ACTION:	The square root of 144 is 14.
BELIEF:	This statement of fact is incorrect
BEHAVIOR:	Consult calculator to determine correct answer.
CONSEQUENCE:	Answer is corrected. The square root of 144 is 12.

However, conflict is not always as simple as this substantive example. Imagine you are in a meeting with your boss and several work associates. During the discussion, you express what you consider a brilliant idea. The discussion continues to circle the table, until it reaches your boss, who recycles your idea. He announces the idea as if it had come to him from a burning bush on Mt. Sinai! Adding insult to your already injured pride, the room erupts in congratulatory praise.

The *Action* in this scenario is your boss taking credit for your idea. However different beliefs may result in different behavior and consequences.

ACTION:	Boss takes credit for your brilliant idea.
BELIEF:	The boss has stolen your idea and you will get no credit for your insight. You are taken for granted. Your boss is a jerk!
BEHAVIOR:	You cannot conceal your emotions. You express frustration to your friends and eventually your boss learns of your dissatisfaction.
CONSEQUENCE:	Your boss thinks you are no longer a team-player. He no longer trusts you to make decisions based on what is best for the company. You are passed over for the promotion you expected.
	OR
ACTION:	Boss takes credit for your brilliant idea.
BELIEF:	The boss has validated you by adopting the idea everyone heard you express. You are proud to have influence over a major policy and glad you expressed yourself.

CONSEQUENCE: The boss confirms you are a team-player and knows you can be trusted to put the company ahead of your personal interests. He puts you at the head of the line for the next promotion.

You cannot control what your boss thinks, says or does. Neither can you control what your spouse, children, co-workers or neighbors think, say or do. However in this relationship conflict, you are able to control your response to the circumstances and the likely consequences: A-B-C.

Some experts use the metaphor of fire to illustrate the effects of conflict. Think of words often used to describe conflict, such as smoldering, burning, flaming, and destructive. Do you see similarities? Fire can also be constructive, sometimes used to burn off underbrush, making land more fertile and productive. Similarly, conflict may bring about positive changes and help empower people.

Certain words, issues or opinions carry the power to ignite conflict. These fuels may also be feelings, like disappointment, anger, humiliation, resentment, envy, fear, contempt, loneliness, inferiority or invisibility. Emotions, lies, faulty perceptions, certain words and phrases may actually serve as accelerants. The more they are poured onto the conflict, the hotter and more destructive it gets. Some of these inflammatory phrases include: "You don't understand," "You don't care!" "I don't care!" "Whatever!" "You're an idiot!" "Shut up!" or "Back off!"

Any firefighter will tell you, fire consists of fuel, oxygen and heat. If you remove any one, you extinguish the fire. If I see an oil fire smoldering in a barrel, I need only to place a lid on top to smother the flames. No oxygen results in no fire.

Similarly, if the accelerant in conflict is an emotion, it is best to start there. "Help me to understand why you are so angry" or "Help me to understand the tears" are good ways to start. If the accelerant is a misunderstanding, try something like, "Help me to understand what you meant when you said you wanted that report as soon as possible."

Unfortunately, we do not generally approach conflict with affirming statements like, "Allow me to tell you who I am. Help me understand who you are. Let's see if we can solve our differences by respecting and appreciating each other." Instead, more often the tendency is to devalue or invalidate the other person. Consequently, one person feels superior, validated or right. The other person feels inferior, invalidated or wrong. Where does he go from there?

"If you disagree with me, you probably disagree with God. Somebody is wrong, but it's not me and God!" It has been my observation that this comment is an unspoken concept in some churches. We faithfully teach children the Golden Rule, *As you would that men should do to you, do ye also to them likewise.* Unfortunately, we have not been so faithful in demonstrating how to apply this noble concept.

We tend to put on our finest clothes and our Sunday smiles, go to church, read our bibles, say our prayers, sing our hymns, go home and eat lunch, take a nap or watch a ballgame. The sermon about the Golden Rule slowly fades. Next week, when we have an opportunity to apply these teachings at work or in traffic or at the shopping mall or grocery store, it's no holds barred and the gloves come off. Praise the Lord!

A lawyer stood up and asked Jesus, *Master, what shall I do to inherit eternal life?* (Luke 10:25-28) Jesus returned the question, no doubt checking to see if the man had been paying attention during recent sermons: *What is written in the law? How do you read it?*

I have always appreciated Jesus' exploratory approach. He not only asked what the law said, he wanted to know how this highly educated professional understood it. *What does it mean to you?* The lawyer demonstrated excellent recall and answered, *Thou shalt love the Lord thy God with all thy heart, and with all thy soul, and with all thy strength, and with all thy mind; and thy neighbor as thyself.* Jesus told the lawyer, "You're absolutely right. You know the words. You recited them perfectly. Now go live by them."

If I believe I should love the Lord my God with all my heart, and with all my soul, and with all my strength, and with all my mind; and my neighbor as myself, then my corresponding behavior will be appropriate to resolving conflict. My behavior will bring consequences, which are redemptive, forgiving, validating, accepting and Christ-like.

Aftermath

A final component of the conflict resolution process is frequently overlooked. Once conflict is settled, often lingering positive or negative thoughts and feelings remain. A clear and decisive defeat often serves to fuel the motive to get even or win next time. Even a compromise may leave participants with an unsettled desire to scrutinize the decision to see if someone actually gained the upper hand. Conversely, effective conflict resolution creates an atmosphere that brings all parties closer together and confident of their compatibility.

While facilitating a meeting of senior executives, I noticed one of the primary participants from the previous discussion appeared unsettled. Her body language suggested she had more to say, but believed the opportunity had passed. I stopped the proceedings and said, "I'm not sure we have completely resolved the previous issue and I'd like to see if there is anything else we need to discuss." As expected, one of the more impatient and aggressive participants declared they had already voted and the matter was closed.

Since my priority was harmony and resolution, I suggested we backtrack for just a few minutes. I asked each participant if they had any other concerns about the prior decision. The troubled executive hesitated and then offered several astute observations, which led the group to conclude their decision had been hasty. Conflict does not go away because we think it should.

It takes a while to gain a clear perspective on the aftermath of any conflict. After a tense and lengthy discussion, your spouse may change her mind about insisting you help with the yard work. She may actually smile and say it is okay for you to go fishing instead. She may even say she hopes you have better luck than *last weekend*. Although it's possible the conflict is resolved, it may have been put on hold until another time. It may be wise to check it out.

Summary

The A-B-C process seems technical and complicated. Actually, it serves as an excellent tool when you need to interrupt the conflict. It allows you to recognize and appreciate the rainbow, instead of remaining overwhelmed by the storm. As you begin to analyze the process, you are no longer fretting, fuming or fussing. You may notice how your beliefs or behavior have contributed to the conflict. It also helps put the potential consequences into perspective, allowing better control over your next crucial step. After all, you want it to be a good one.

NINE

SYMPTOMS OF CONFLICT

Sitting in the darkness of my study, scrambled voices echoed in my troubled thoughts. As I looked into the shadowy stillness, all I could see was the flashing of the digital clock on my desk, reminding me in bright red numerals it was 3:35am. Occasionally the squeaking of my chair, which I could never seem to find the time to repair, interrupted the silence, drawing me back from my distant thoughts. For the most part, I just watched the ever-changing digits on the clock, wondering how my life, my ministry had arrived at this point. Had it all been the will of God? When God called me to become a pastor, had he intended my ministry to collide with the cold hard brutality of human nature at this place, at this time?

I asked myself what we would do for income if we left the church. The capacity to read New Testament Greek did not seem such a hot commodity for the struggling job market! The church also provided our house. Where would we live if asked to leave? Would these people with whom we had shared so many special times really kick us out on the street?

We had seemed so close through the years. If a crisis arose, they did not hesitate to call, even in the middle of the night. I served them communion, baptized their children and ate their horrible rhubarb pie. They wept in my arms in times of peril or loss. Did they no longer see me as the man they were once so positive God had sent their way?

As the minutes clicked away, I began to feel the fatigue of the past twenty-four hours. I recalled the beautiful weddings. I remembered the funerals. They were never easy. I could still hear a deacon's voice stinging with hostilities from earlier in the evening, while recalling the tears rolling down his rugged cheeks as we watched his mother's casket lowering into the ground.

I remembered long hours of waiting in hospital rooms, anxious to hear only brief words of encouragement, while certain we were deep into the shadows of death. Sometimes the right words came and sometimes only a painful silence. What seemed most important was holding on to each other when we need it most. Or was it?

The efficient little digits reminded me again of the late hour. It was 4:21am. I could still feel the churning of my stomach from the Deacon's Meeting. I felt the weight of fatigue becoming heavier with each passing moment. Perhaps I had waited long enough. Maybe now I had reached the familiar point of exhaustion that would allow me to fall into bed, finally able to sleep.

Sleep had become my greatest ally…when it would come. It meant no more worries, no more arguments and no more opportunities for my thoughts to haunt me. However, the virtual certainty of tomorrow meant more of the same dreary, anxious existence.

Over the weeks of conflict, I had begun to question my ability to lead and counsel. I even questioned my identity, my call into the ministry. Why were people so cruel? What could I have done differently? Could I have chosen my words with better discernment? Where was God in all of this?

One morning, after another troubled night with only a few hours sleep, I stood in front of the bathroom mirror, looking into dark empty eyes with the most frightening thought, "Good grief. That's me!"[2]

These are the images and thoughts of a pastor in conflict. However, they could be images of anyone, at any time, in any profession. They represent symptoms of internalized conflict.

Suppose you go to your family doctor with symptoms of a chills and fever, head congestion, body aches, fatigue and nausea. It probably will not require a great diagnostician to diagnose the flu, promptly sending you home with antibiotics and instructions for bed rest. The symptoms illustrated in the preceding story also lead to a diagnosis. The sufferer describes frequent insomnia, while replaying embattled conversations. He describes frequent worry and anxiety. As anyone about to lose his job, he wonders how he will support his family or pay his bills. He also has begun to question his identity and self worth. Conflict, much like a physical illness, often causes recognizable symptoms, not easily resolved without the necessary care.

The church is a place where we say our prayers, sing our hymns and celebrate our individual relationship with Almighty God. However, all too often, where two or three are gathered, there is too much conflict to bring tenderness and healing. This reality has the potential for life altering consequences.

A unique drama tends to play out when pastors lose their churches. Almost universally, pastors believe God calls them into ministry. They go to seminary to study things like Greek, Hebrew and hermeneutics. However when people or circumstances, even beyond their control, cause them to leave this divine calling, their identity is greatly compromised. The pastor in the previous crisis is not afraid of losing his job as much as he is afraid of losing himself.

Similarly, a husband and father may find his identity threatened when conflict at work causes him to lose his job, then a worsening economy prevents him from returning to his chosen profession. He may feel less of a man because he can no longer adequately provide for his family. He may feel guilt or shame for losing his job and become very angry with the people or circumstances separating him from his employment. He may question his role as a husband or father. He may eventually find a new job, but still be missing a part of himself.

Symptoms are physical, emotional and spiritual reactions used to identify conflict and to bring resolution. It is important to understand that symptoms are only indicators. A sniffle may be a symptom of a chronic cocaine addiction. It may also indicate your husband is allergic to the roses he just bought home. A little common sense can go a long way.

WITHDRAWAL AND ISOLATION

Conflict has many symptoms and some are very subtle. Withdrawal is a frequently overlooked symptom of conflict, especially in churches.

Pastors, deacons, Sunday school teachers, ministers of music, and a host of other leaders, frequently notice when faithful church members are absent. A familiar pew or chair is empty. A warm familiar handshake does not come. What a brilliant way to draw the pastor into their home for a visit! Then during conversation over coffee and cookies, their concerned minister learns the details of their latest conflict.

Withdrawal is just as easy to find in the home, office, or garden club. Suppose your teenage daughter becomes angry when not allowed to go out with her friends. She retreats into her room, slamming the door just loud enough so everyone hears, but not loud enough to get Dad out of his chair. She comes to breakfast as everyone else is finishing, presumably after oversleeping. She silently stares out the window during the car ride to school. She has effectively withdrawn.

Perhaps you and Dave have a disagreement over an office project. Dave is a capable programmer, with definite ideas about making the project flow smoothly. His ideas also make life easier for Dave! On the other hand, you have a broader perspective on the office's objectives and prefer taking another approach. While trying to schedule another meeting, Dave indicates frequent conflicts with the dates and times you recommend. Finally, the meeting is scheduled and the electronic invitations sent. You arrive with your notes and have your thoughts together, but there is no Dave! Finally, after everyone is seated and quiet, he ambles into the room, ten minutes late.

Withdrawal is not always as obvious as saying, "I'm taking my toys and going home!" It may be as simple as *not* expressing an opinion during a group discussion, changing the subject, diverting a group from the task at hand or arriving late. It may be as subtle as walking past a colleague's office, not saying "hello" or checking your emails from the office, while your in-laws are visiting in the other room.

SELF-JUSTIFICATION

Do you know anyone who thinks he is never wrong? Do you know anyone who simply cannot apologize? Many times these characteristics come from unspoken insecurities, which shape their relationships. Remember, most people do not like conflict, but want it resolved to their personal satisfaction. To justify a conflicting perspective, some choose to enhance their own superiority. They remind us to "look at what you made me do!"

Personal and *moral superiority* tend to blend easily with *self-justification*. Edie and Alice worked together for decades. Through the years, they watched several bosses come and go. They all arrived with big, innovative plans, but soon drifted back to reality when none of their ideas worked.

One day, the two colleagues were in the Break Room discussing a new policy posted on the bulletin board. A co-worker entered, read the new policy, turned to Edie and Alice and said, "This really sounds great. What a neat idea!" Edie whispered to Alice, "She hasn't been here long enough to realize how bad that idea really is."

Sometimes new members of an office team, professional group or Sunday school class find it hard to be taken seriously until establishing *tenure*. Of course, tenure is determined by different, sometimes unspoken standards.

Were you ever the new kid in class? How did it feel? Your mistakes were probably exaggerated and your accomplishments short-changed to keep you humble. Most likely even your good ideas were received with a snicker. Of course, if you said or did something bringing accolades to the "in-crowd," you were likely brought under their umbrella of acceptance. It might have taken a week, month, or more, but eventually you passed the unwritten, but clearly understood, length of time required before they stopped saying, "He hasn't been here long enough."

Moral superiority easily gains ground in church conflict, because it potentially carries the approval of God. If I come to a meeting, which promises to be filled with conflicting opinions and a close vote, is it not to my advantage to begin my remarks with, "Last night I prayed until midnight and woke up this morning believing we should ...." If God is on my side, who should dare be against me?

Self-justification and superiority create symptoms opposite from withdrawal. They push people away who do not agree. They assert, "If you do not agree with my perspective, you do not belong!" Usually, these are symptoms of individuals who have previously felt the sting of confrontation, change, disagreement or having been declared wrong.

In response, they have chosen to cultivate alliances based on the justification of their perspective.

DENIAL

Denial is hard to detect, because it tends to be so subtle. It is equally hard to resolve. Katrina is a naturally gregarious person. She has never met a person with whom she did not want to talk! She is a people-person, who loves her work as a receptionist. She talks on the phone, emails, and chats with customers as soon as they walk in the door. She likes people and needs to be liked! When Katrina is in conflict, she promptly tucks it away. She believes nice people do not have conflict. She smiles, changes the subject and avoids confrontation at all costs.

One day, Morgan asked Katrina if she had ordered some material he needed for a meeting the next week. She had not. Morgan had asked her to order the material two weeks earlier. He became frustrated with her procrastination and sternly instructed her to do it immediately!

As Katrina prepared the purchase orders needed for Morgan's meeting, Joe stepped into her doorway. "Wow. Sounds like you're not Morgan's favorite person today!" Katrina smiled broadly and said, "You know, Morgan and I are such good friends. He gets upset like that when he's under pressure. He just needs to get some rest before that big meeting."

Katrina did not accept that Morgan's frustration pointed directly at her work ethic. He may have been under pressure, but this conflict flared because of Katrina's procrastination. It was not about her. It was about her behavior. Her failure to realize this may lead to greater frustrations. From Morgan's perspective, their relationship also suffered from a loss of trust. He may eventually perceive Katrina's actions as a potential sabotage of his meeting.

Katrina did not acknowledge conflict existed with Morgan. She believed this was nothing more than a petty disagreement between friends. If Katrina elects not to acknowledge the conflict, she does not have to feel its emotional intensity. Consequently, she remains free to talk more with Joe and order the material later.

Another component of Katrina's denial is in her need to be liked by everyone. When Joe came to her office, she did not want to admit

Morgan did not like her. She simply deflected his concern with a flippant explanation of Morgan's uneasiness over the anticipated meeting.

Similarly, church members sometimes attend worship, cloaked in unresolved conflict, flaring emotions and troubled thoughts. If I believe good Christians do not get angry or have disagreements, my behavior might falsely indicate I am in complete agreement with you. However, my outward denial is only a façade hiding my real thoughts and feelings. The handshakes may be warm and friendly, but the lines of disagreement may be drawn already. This cheapens the diversity of the decision-making process and diminishes my contribution.

Sometimes husbands and wives in conflict also prefer denial. The belief that conflict will resolve itself, frequently leads to unfortunate consequences. A small argument today and a broken promise tomorrow may lead to resentments and harsher arguments down the road. Eventually, he withdraws to televised ball games and sophisticated video games. She withdraws to home shows and tennis lessons. Eventually the withdrawal and indifference are justified and casually explained away as merely the result of too many years of familiarity. However, this behavior may represent symptoms of unresolved conflict, temporarily held by denial in a secure, comfortable place. If ignored for long, it will metastasize into something potently deadly for their marriage.

DISRESPECTFUL COMMUNICATION

The most obvious examples of this symptom are sarcasm, personal attacks or quick-tempered sniping. Abrupt outspokenness is often a disguised symptom of unresolved conflict, which may conceal feelings of neglect, rejection, powerlessness or frustration.

Sheila had worked in a large corporation for several decades and was nearing retirement. She generally socialized with co-workers, with whom she had been friends for years. She was often the lone voice of dissention during staff meetings. She frequently wrote complaint memos to or about upper management and had a knack for causing old problems to resurface.

A closer examination reveals management often overlooked Sheila for promotions and salary increases. She believed her excellent job performance had gone unappreciated and her position underestimated for its impact. She felt unnoticed and devalued. She used her outspokenness to announce herself. It also indicated unresolved anger and recurrent internalized conflict. Because management had become too preoccupied to diagnose Sheila's symptoms as anything but bitterness, they labeled her a problem employee. Consequently, her frustration and abrupt outspokenness became more intense, resulting in personnel actions.

NAME CALLING

We learned this tactic in the Second Grade, but we still like to call people names when we dislike them. It was cute when we heard things like "Jerry, Jerry, he's a dingle berry," teacher's pet, tattle tale, or four-eyes. However, with added sophistication, our name-calling became less humorous with names like dork, nerd, loser, slut, and skank. Even today's political lexicon contains acceptable names for adversaries such as, liberal, conservative, socialist, fundamentalist, flip-flopper, maverick and birther.

As a symptom of a greater problem, this tactic rarely occurs in face-to-face confrontations. Two co-workers in the office Break Room may refer to their boss as a *buffoon* or another co-worker as a *slob* or accuse her of kissing up to management. These comments, used to devalue the other individual or undermine management are symptomatic of greater differences within the office environment. They possibly mask anger, bitterness, resentment, envy, jealousy or a host of other more serious symptoms.

In the parking lot following worship, a deacon may comment, "I wish he would just start preaching the Bible!" The implication being the pastor has said something unpopular and the parking lot crowd has labeled it unbiblical. We do the same thing in the secular world when we label people un-American or unpatriotic because we disagree over politics. However, the comment is merely symptomatic of a greater conflict reaching much deeper than the parking lot or Board Room.

SILENCE IS NOT ALWAYS GOLDEN

Imagine Ernest and Esther in their home one evening. Usually dinner consists of a lively discussion of the day's events, but tonight there was very little conversation. As customary, Ernest retires to the den for television, while Esther remains in the kitchen.

Increasing the volume a second time, Ernest realizes the clashing of pots and pans, and slamming cabinet doors have interrupted his television show. Only moderately curious about the distraction, Ernest called to the other room, "Peaches, is everything okay?" Esther called back, "Everything is just fine," then mumbles something he cannot quite make out.

Ernest continues clicking the remote, searching for his favorite television show, barely noticing Esther has breezed behind his chair on her way to the bedroom. On her return trip, he caught the obvious sigh and heavy stomping. During the first commercial break, Ernest again called out to Esther, "Honey, what's wrong?" She curtly replies, "Nothing!"

Esther may not have been completely silent, but she was not saying anything! At least, she was not communicating her feelings to Ernest in ways he could understand. Her silence, accompanied by slamming doors, rattling pots and pans, sighs and foot stomping were symptoms of conflict.

Esther is one of the best cooks in town. She takes great pride in her prize winning cakes and pies. A later conversation would reveal Esther became angry when Ernest arrived home late without calling, causing her roast to dry out in the oven. Her feelings intensified when he commented her roast "wasn't as juicy as last time." Esther's noisy silence served only as a symptom of the conflict resting just beneath the surface. Her roast would have been tender and juicy if he had come home on time! His insensitive comment struck sharply at her self-worth. How dare he?

Silence is a companion symptom with withdrawal. For example, a church member may choose to leave worship by another door, avoiding contact with the pastor. A teenage son may withdraw into video games or music, retreating into a world requiring no verbal interaction. A co-worker may send an email proudly announcing the birth of a grandchild, but receive no response from a colleague with whom she has had a recent disagreement. Silence is counter-productive and sometimes destructive when used to conceal conflict.

EMOTIONS

Emotions are likely the most obvious symptom of conflict. To ignore them is like building your house on a foundation of sand. Fear, anger, powerlessness, grief, loneliness, bitterness, apprehension, anxiety, mistrust, resentment, aloneness, humiliation and depression are only a few labels for the monumental impact emotions have on conflict resolution.

A key rule in resolving interpersonal conflict is to address emotions before anything else. Tears must be dried and fists unclenched. You cannot communicate effectively through gritted teeth and you cannot work out solutions if you are too angry to see straight. Emotions are neither logical nor reasonable, neither good nor bad, neither sinful nor holy. Feelings are facts and highly relevant to conflict. Deal with them!

While preparing to grill steaks on the deck one evening, I carried a large plate containing several steaks, my tongs, a bottle of olive oil and a roll of paper towels. Approaching the back door, I realized I had no available resource to open it. Of course, I could have put it down, opened the door…that was too easy! I tucked the paper towels under my chin, balanced the heavy plate on one arm and reached to open the door. As the door opened, I dropped the tongs. I reached down to pick up the tongs. While straightening, I failed to notice the door had come farther ajar. It was a head to door collision! Recoiling from the injury, I again dropped the tongs. While turning to pick up the tongs, the plate tipped and a steak slid to the floor. My brilliant solution was to kick the door. Yes, I became angry and kicked an inanimate object! Sound familiar?

Symptoms of conflict come in many packages, with differing interpretations. They may seem intimidating or sometimes unimportant and remain unnoticed. However, ignoring these symptoms is like shooting an arrow, then drawing the target. Like Ernest watching television after dinner, conflict may be resolved to our own personal satisfaction. We have hit our target! However, Ernest failed to realize Esther had her own target and he missed it by a mile! Effectively resolving interpersonal conflict requires drawing the target, aiming the bow and firing the arrow together.

TEN

PERSONALITIES

Personality differences carry the potential for unexpected complications. Curiously, the same event or circumstance may cause conflict for one person and not another. Missing a business deadline by two days may be upsetting, physically and emotionally, to an individual who has spent a professional lifetime being on time, meeting goals, and living by a prescribed set of standards. Another individual, who faces each day spontaneously, may be relieved to have come so close! Consequently, conflict often has a very personal dynamic.

Our personalities are crafted as family genetics blend with personal experiences. As we learn (or not) from our mistakes, gain new insights, experience different cultures, emotionally and intellectually mature, hopefully we become more aware of who we are and how we are perceived by others. However, when our unique personality is called to interact with another unique personality, the potential for conflict is heightened.

Personality differences often cause us to wonder and worry. Will she find me reserved and shy or think I am conceited? Will he think I am an organized professional or a control freak? Will she think I am cold and indifferent or logical and objective? Will he think I am assertive or argumentative and demanding?

Understanding how personalities work is complicated business. Our pugs, Tess and Riley, illustrate how specific differences are obvious, even in animals. Tess gets up each morning at her customary time and has a prescribed routine. She goes outside promptly and expects breakfast prepared when she returns. Following breakfast, she returns to her bed, awaiting the next series of events. When Teri calls, "Kennel Time," she jumps from the bed and runs into her kennel cage. She expects a treat in return for her cooperation!

Upon arriving home each afternoon, we open the kennel and Tess runs to the back door, anticipating another treat when she returns. She knows when to expect dinner and like a senior citizen accustomed to the *Five-O'clock Special*, does not like delays. During the evening, she lounges in her favorite chair, patiently waiting for another trip outside and bedtime. She may elect to chase an airplane on its final approach to a nearby airport, but generally any departure from this routine is unusual.

Riley is more laid-back. He gets up according to Tess's internal clock. He pounces from bed and runs to the door, but would stay outside and chase squirrels, if Tess did not return to the back door. He eats breakfast, because pugs will always eat! Instead of going straight to bed, he waits around to see if any other action is on tap. He also goes into the kennel on command, but not as much out of routine as for the treat. At the end of the day, he is also ready to go outside, but takes the evening's events in stride: get a treat, bark at the neighbor's cat, help Mom with the laundry, supervise Dad at the computer and watch television.

During the evening, while Tess quietly observes, Riley remains busy. He chases dogs, cats, raccoons and other animals in television commercials. He barks and jumps at the television, then demands to go outside, expecting to find the television animal on the deck. Frustrated over finding no playmate, he jumps at the doorknob, trying to come back inside. His evening is generally action-packed, including a revolving series of exits and returns.

Television and movies have cashed in on these types of personality differences. The persnickety Felix Unger is placed opposite spontaneous, unkempt Oscar Madison in Neil Simon's play, *The Odd Couple*. Finicky Alan Harper clashes with his brother Charley's free-wheeling unpredictable lifestyle in *Two and a Half Men*[3]. Theoretical Physicist, Sheldon Cooper, in *The Big Bang Theory*[4], maintains a fastidiously regimented routine for everything, including his personal seat on the couch, dumbfounding his next door neighbor, Penny, who rarely cleans her apartment.

INTROVERTS AND EXTROVERTS

Some people live in a world of thoughts, ideas and understanding. We call them *Introverts*[5]. Like an iceberg, they reveal very little of themselves, until developing a strong bond of trust. Consequently, we perceive them as shy, reserved, impenetrable or conceited.

An introvert's preferred communication style is impersonal. Texting, email, voicemail, letters and notes attached to refrigerators or computer monitors are generally preferred to the telephone. As children, they prefer talking to mirrors, animals, dolls or imaginary friends than people. They may enjoy singing, but while alone in their bedroom or car, not in a karaoke bar. Abraham Lincoln and Albert Einstein were introverts. I also suspect Moses may have been an introvert, since he spent so much time wandering around alone in obscure mountains and talking to shrubbery.

However, introvertedness has very little to do with social skills. I am a minister, lecturer and business executive. I am also an introvert. I am trained to speak publically and to engage an audience. I enjoy making lengthy presentations to large crowds and conducting workshops. However, my energy is recharged by being alone with my thoughts. During a lunch break, I may retreat into a quiet room or have lunch alone to re-charge for the next session. At the end of the day, I usually feel drained. Instead of a night on the town with acquaintances, I prefer a brisk walk or retreat into television situation comedies.

Introverts are driven by their thoughts. Consequently, having the right idea is important. We think before we speak, sometimes causing us to be overlooked or forgotten. We tend to have a characteristic pause, which may incorrectly suggest we have nothing to say. Frequently, Teri will ask me a question and receive no immediate reply. Assuming I did not hear, she repeats the question. However, I have heard her. I am still thinking!

Introverts usually prefer listening to talking, unless the subject is one with which we have exceptional familiarity. At parties we prefer interactions with a few individuals, with whom we can build a brief rapport, rather than floating from person to person. We may have many acquaintances, but few close friends, because we do not easily welcome you inside! We appear to have a "closed door" policy at work, but this is usually because we prefer working alone, not to be antisocial. We are also terrible with names. I once clipped pictures and names from a church directory and used them as flash cards to learn the membership of a new congregation.

In contrast, *Extroverts* live in a loud world of sounds, conversations and activities. Like big colorful hot-air balloons, they drift over their landscape searching for new, exciting places to land. They appear affable and relaxed in social surroundings. They like to work with others and become recharged through group activities. They appear to have an "open door" policy, but may get easily drawn off task by frequent distractions. They sometimes give the illusion of being intellectually superficial, because their comments seem inconsistent and disorganized. However, while introverts think before speaking, an extrovert speaks in order to think. What you hear them saying may not be their final answer! It may be only today's edition.

If an introvert talks about taking a trip to New York City, he has likely had this idea for a good while and possibly researched air fares and hotel accommodations. If an extrovert talks about a trip to New York City, she likely means New York City is an exciting city and one of the many places she hopes to go one day, when the time and resources are right.

If you want to know what an extrovert is thinking, just ask or listen for a few minutes. If you want to know what the introvert is thinking, ask, and a day or two later, she will give you her most conclusive answer.

Franklin D. Roosevelt and Theodore Roosevelt were extroverts. I believe King David also had similar characteristics. He sang, danced in the streets, wearing a linen apron that left his backside exposed and seemed to have a charismatic personality.

Under stress, an introvert tends to withdraw even deeper until erupting in a display of surprising behavior. An extrovert tends to unload emotions and troubling thoughts as they go along. Extroverts will get louder and more distracted, but the introvert is more noticeable, primarily because her behavior appears so uncharacteristic.

Introverts and extroverts also handle conflict differently. Introverts keep most of their thoughts and feelings internalized. When an introverted spouse says she wants a divorce, these thoughts undoubtedly have been germinating for weeks or more. This type of conflict is hard to resolve because the introvert is generally so far ahead of everyone else. They have internalized the struggle, possibly for weeks and have become reconciled to the decision. On the other hand, the extrovert will have given hundreds of signals of brewing problems and can say without fear of contradiction, "I told you so!"

SOME PEOPLE ARE MORE CONCRETE THAN OTHERS

Some people take rules and instructions to a higher level than others. When we say people are concrete, we mean they do not easily move beyond what appears *carved in stone*. If a recipe calls for ¼ cup of white wine, that is all it gets! They eat breakfast, because experts say it is the most important meal of the day and fill out forms only with the prescribed #2 pencil.

Teri and Sandra, who are very good friends and business colleagues, went to lunch at a local fast food restaurant. They arrived long after the lunch crowd had left, leaving the spacious counter open and available. Sandra walked directly to the cash register to place her order. Wondering why Teri was not nearby, Sandra turned to find her walking through the obviously empty queue line. In disbelief, Sandra demanded to know why she had not walked directly to the counter. Teri paused then laughed, "People are supposed to walk through the queue line when they order. That is the rule!"

Some people perceive the world around them based on their five senses. They believe only what they see, touch, smell, taste or hear. If it looks like a duck, quacks like a duck, walks like a duck and says its name is Donald, it must be a duck! They have a good eye for details and make good accountants and bankers. They follow rules and make good police officers. They prefer art that conveys realism, such as a landscape or portrait. If you ask them to talk about apples, they may mention Granny Smith, Golden Delicious, and Winesap. They might also mention apples were first served as dessert in ancient Greece and come from the species Malus Domestica. They will enjoy this type of book because it provides instructions.

Other people perceive the world around them through the discernment of patterns. They prefer possibilities and theories over facts. They use their imagination and hunches to form global perspectives. They make good professors, counselors, and medical diagnosticians. They enjoy abstract art and novels that leave something to the imagination. If you ask them to talk about apples, they might mention Isaac Newton and the theory of gravity, computers, and the Garden of Eden. They will enjoy this type of book because it offers new alternatives and stimulates thought.

My mother perceives the world factually. She lives by rules and expects her rules followed to the letter. Undoubtedly, she would have followed Teri through the restaurant queue! I tend to be more creative and abstract. I played with imaginary friends and preferred theology over accounting.

When I was a teenager, my mother enforced a rule that stirred relentless conflict. She believed my clothes were either clean or dirty. I should hang them up or throw them in the hamper. It seemed simple.

Many decades later, she still does not understand my belief that clothes, especially jeans, have varying degrees of dirtiness. Sometimes, they are too clean to go into the hamper, but not clean enough to go back into the closet. The back of a chair or foot of the bed seems to provide a more suitable interim space.

Since my mother is nearing eighty years of age, I will likely not change her perspective. Basically, we agree to disagree. It is often wise to pick your battles, instead of allowing personality differences to cause unnecessary complications in meaningful relationships. C'est la vie!

ORGANIZATION OR SPONTANEITY?

Do you remember Tina and her supervisor, Barbie? It was end of the day and Tina was shutting down her computer, preparing for the weekend. Barbie stuck her head in the doorway, displaying a sheepish grin, "Teeee'na, I know it's been a long day and you're ready to go home, but we need to put our heads together about this project." She waved several blank pages in Tina's direction. Tina gathered her purse and looked up, "Uh, what project is that?" Barbie looked at the blank pages and giggled, "Oh, not this. You know that survey senior management asked us to prepare." Tina rolled her chair back from her computer, "Which survey is that?" Barbie responded, "You didn't get the email? Oh, let me send that to you." Tina stood up, "Barbie, I'm on my way out. Is this something that can wait until Monday? When does management need the survey?" Barbie answered, "Oh, I didn't see a deadline. Let me go back and read it again."

Tina needs structure, organization, specific details, clear expectations and respect for her values. Her day is planned precisely. She allows a specific amount of time for each meeting and project. She carefully reads and responds to emails and voicemails daily. Her business calendar is meticulously accurate for the next several months.

Tina plans her personal life with equal precision. When planning a vacation, she makes hotel and airline reservations months in advance. She plans each day's events, including meals, recreational activities and transportation. She decides what she needs to do and gets it done!

People like Tina prefer settling issues quickly and decisively. Consequently, they sometimes make decisions prematurely. This is not a problem unless they refuse to reconsider new facts, listen to proposed alternatives or believe reconsidering is a weakness.

Barbie considers herself more adaptable than Tina. She sees herself as curious and open-minded. She prefers to keep her options open until the last minute. Her vacation trips are more spontaneous, so she can enjoy the unexpected. She begins working on projects just before their due date, because she works better under pressure. Her day is cluttered with personal phone calls, meetings, lunch dates, and sorting through hundreds of unread emails, but she prefers it flexible, not scheduled and boring. Tina perceives this lack of preparation and spontaneity as incompetency.

These personality differences are not uncommon. Tina will stay in constant internalized conflict and increasingly resent Barbie's spontaneous supervisory style. Barbie will perceive Tina as progressively rigid, intolerant and annoying. Until they take time to discuss and understand their differences, these tensions will continue to complicate their relationship. Once Barbie realizes Tina's personality characteristics can help her become more effective, balancing her spontaneity with some needed organization, her department may become remarkably productive. Personality differences do not have to cause problems. They simply bring complications that should be recognized and addressed promptly.

DECISION MAKING

We tend to use our thoughts or feelings to make our final decisions. Some will not buy a new car without surveying the literature and canvassing several dealers to determine the best price, options and package. Others go into a car dealership, not certain what they want, but marvel that the first car they see is their favorite shade of blue. They make their decision because it feels right! Of course, these are extremes, but demonstrate how decisions are generally made.

Some of us are sentimental, tactful, and need to be liked. Others are logical, factual and could not care less if they are liked. You can usually tell if you are talking with thinking or feeling-oriented individuals by simply asking them about their weekend. A thinking-oriented person will give you a brief, logical synopsis of the weekend's high and low points. They do not intend to be abrupt or matter of fact, but their answer will follow a logical sequence. A feeling-oriented person will provide you a colorfully detailed panoramic description of their trip to the grocery market! Conflict between these two personalities is not easily resolved and may bring tears and acrimony, possibly even alimony!

People who make decisions by logic and thought processes, tend to express themselves critically or skeptically. They make critical observations, not to get a response, but because they consider them factual and worth mentioning. A gentler, sensitive individual may overhear these abrupt comments, misunderstand the intent and his feelings may be unintentionally hurt.

Sometimes logical, intellectual people appear defensive or argumentative, especially to others who need harmony and agreement. Sometimes thinking-oriented people have trouble expressing or understanding their feelings and need someone to guide them. Conversely, since feelings are linked to our values, sometimes logic is needed to calm emotions and restore order.

William is a highly educated man with proven success in his career. He is married to Carmen with two children in their twenties. His personality is reserved and quiet, but he is polished enough to socialize comfortably. He discusses issues of interest with a passion, but tends to make decisions intellectually. Carmen is also a well-educated professional. She is talkative and responds more to her feelings.

They rarely argue. Their personalities are similar and they have come to understand each other through the years. However, one evening they disagreed over a seemingly unimportant matter. William became unusually passionate and animated. He began to raise his voice, not as much to overpower Carmen, but to emphasize his opinion. Carmen made the mistake of suggesting he should "Calm down." This struck a nerve.

William sees himself as reasonable, logical, introspective and sometimes passionate, but always under control. Carmen's request shot across the bow of his self perception! How dare she insinuate he was anything but composed? If he had become unusually zealous in citing his position, it was because she was obstinate and not listening. He was certainly not fanatical or in need of sedation as her comment implied!

Carmen did not intend to accelerate the conflict or imply he needed sedation. She innocently used a phrase that unintentionally attacked William's self-esteem. His perception of her statement, irrational as it may have been, intensified the argument unnecessarily.

William and Carmen demonstrate how easily personality issues can draw a simple conversation into an argument. Introverted people need time to think things through before expressing an opinion. Extroverts need a safe place to think out loud, without being judged. People who use their senses to perceive the world, want to get their hands dirty and experience life. Others wonder what kind of world exists outside the Garden. Tina and Barbie will not find peace until they accept their differences, not as potential conflict, but as an opportunity.

People are different and sometimes profoundly annoying, yet created by the capricious imagination of God to live in this crowded world together. Sometimes our differences seem immeasurable. Harmony and reconciliation appear beyond our grasp. However, in the beginning, God said, "Let there be light," and an entire universe was brought out of darkness. Surely, that kind of creative power can illuminate a twinkle of compatibility and understanding within the shadows of your conflict. So, let not your hearts be troubled; believe in God.

ELEVEN

COMMUNICATION

Upon arrival at the Southern Baptist Theological Seminary in 1979, I entered a world unlike anywhere else. The seminary was a place of intellectual reverence, where Greek and Hebrew were studied in pursuit of greater spiritual insights. Students learned to write and preach sermons not speeches. I thought of it as hallowed ground on which to seek the word and presence of God.

One day in the library, I discovered there were those who took their pursuit of theology with less reverence. While researching an assignment, I found a note jotted on a piece of ragged paper, apparently used as a bookmark. It referred to Jesus as he traveled with his disciples through the villages of Caesarea Philippi. He asked, "Who do men say that I am?" Before Simon Peter offered the correct answer, another disciple blurted, "You are the divine presupposition of our sacerdotal functions, our supreme spiritual eschatological manifestation; you are he who overcomes our existential estrangement." Jesus stopped, turned around and said "Huh?"

I think this slam on intellectual sophistication existed in theological schools long before I arrived. It still survives on the internet and around the world in various revisions. It also remains a stunning reminder that the words we use have a direct impact on our relationships. I may have the same perspective as you, but if I express myself in terms you do not understand, we may not realize we are on the same page or we may never get there! When Relationship Conflict is complicated by ineffective communication, it has as much to do with what is heard, understood and perceived as with the words themselves.

If I collect two, three or a hundred people who are in conflict and ask them what they need most to resolve their differences, a single phrase tends to draw their broken relationships into perspective: better communication. With little more than a whisper, words can encourage, heal, instruct, praise and affirm. They can just as easily disappoint, humiliate, discourage, infuriate or alienate you from someone who needs you most.

Communication seems simple. We do it every day. But, is it so simple? Jesus spoke in parables. God communicated through burning shrubbery, dreams, angels, and sometimes wrote on walls. When he gave Moses the Ten Commandments on Mt. Sinai, God not only wrote them down, he carved them in stone! We live in a culture cluttered with communication tools: the internet, wireless internet, email, and a spectrum of hand-held electronic devices. We twitter and text thousands of times a day. Yet, with these cutting-edge tools at our fingertips, communication remains a stumbling block.

How often do we fail to hear what is really being said beyond the spoken word? Will you notice the tear on a co-worker's cheek as she assures you everything is fine? Do you know what she really means when your daughter says her life is over...at least for the moment? When your boss says to get a project completed as soon as possible, how will you know he means *today*?

When you meet someone for the first time, what do you notice immediately? You likely notice their flare for fashion, hair, eyes, smile, or how they carry themselves, but probably not their words! Researchers tell us only about seven percent of all communication comes from our words. The rest is non-verbal communication such as tone, emphasis, posture, facial expressions and other body language. Teri may ask, "Ken, are you going to mow the lawn?" and depending on her tone, it can sound like a simple inquiry or a command. Researchers even study micro-expressions to understand the deeper meanings in a person's words.

Our use of words is an interesting complication to conflict. Perhaps that explains why St. Francis of Assisi once said, "Preach the Gospel at all times and when necessary use words."

AMBIGUITIES

Sometimes we fail to say what we mean or to make ourselves clear. Phrases like, "It's not very far," "I'll be there in a minute," or "Let's do lunch" require interpretation. Each phrase has to be put into specific context. A five-mile trip may not be very far if I am driving a car, but what if I am walking? Suppose Donald Trump and Bill Gates are discussing a purchase and one says to the other "It doesn't cost much." That statement may mean something very different if you and I had a similar conversation.

Familiar phrases like, "I love you," "I don't care," or "Whatever you want to do," may mean something different to the speaker, than to the hearer. The emotions woven into each comment also need interpretation. An effective communicator invests a great deal of effort in reducing the possibility of ambiguity.

One day Supervisor Barbie visited Sam, a member of the company Information Technology staff. Sheepishly entering his office, she said in a buttery smooth tone, "Sam, I'm in a pickle. I need you to re-format the Craig Brochure. The boss doesn't think it looks professional enough." She knew Sam was good-natured and had a hard time refusing. As expected, Sam replied, "Sure. I have a project to finish this afternoon, but I can do that before I go home. What format do you want me to use?" Barbie smiled as she usually did when she had no idea what to say, "Oh, you know these things better than I. Just go to the company website and choose the one you think works best."

Sam finished his original project and worked until eight o'clock that evening, using the company website to re-format the Craig Brochure. He did not like to sacrifice family time, but he thought he should do his best to get Barbie out of a *pickle*. The next morning she called, "Sam, what did you do? I'm afraid this brochure just won't work. It has to be more professional. Management just won't like this!" Sam sighed heavily and told her he had gone to the website and selected a design just as she had asked. She replied, "Oh Sam, you know I meant for you to go to the Marketing page. You got this from the Human Resources page. This just won't do." Sam paused and took deep breath, "Barbie, I stayed late just to help you out. I won't have time to work on this again until the end of the week." She sternly replied, "Well, if you had done it right the first time we wouldn't be having this conversation." Sam answered, "I've got work to do. The next time you need a favor, please try to have a clue before you call me!"

Actually, Sam did not know Barbie meant for him to get the format from the Marketing page. She had delegated the task to him with only vague instructions. He stayed late to help her and received only criticism in return. Barbie's anxiety over likely not getting the corrections to management on time created more tension. Her unclear instructions had led to the original misunderstanding. Her insensitivity and stern words made it worse. Their relationship was in conflict.

OVER-GENERALIZATIONS

Some people tend to speak in exaggerations. When your wife says, "You *never* listen" what does she want you to hear? If a colleague says you are *always* late, is that statement based on facts or a perception? If your girlfriend says you *never* let her go out with her friends, is she stating fact or a perception based on the last time it came up? Seldom are these over-generalizations true. People may be consistent, predictable or even obsessive, but the words *always* and *never* seldom ring true. If Teri says "Ken never eats liver," she may think her statement is factual. However, she is unaware of the time my grandfather convinced me to eat liver, insisting it was actually *bear meat*.

Suppose you are attending a Flower Club meeting and someone says, "Everyone likes our new pastor!" Is that statement fact or perception? The scoop in her social circle may indicate the new pastor is well liked, but does she speak for *everyone*? Has she heard the latest report from the local garage, the high school, the town restaurants and the bar at the Country Club? She may know that some or many or most people like the new pastor. She may even think he is the best pastor ever! However, her statement is an over-generalization, based on her perception of the pastor's popularity.

The same is true when signs indicate *No one* likes the new pastor. These over-generalizations are intended to give value to an individual perspective, but seldom have much credible level of validation. They tend to add complications to conflict by stirring insecurities or suspicion.

MIXED MESSAGES

Sometimes what you do not say, speaks volumes! If you ask your teenage son if he has taken the garbage to the curb and get a nod (up and down), you have a general idea what he means. If he shakes his head (side to side), you also understand his simple, although impolite communication. This is not the case in other parts of the world, where these gestures mean just the opposite.

If I place the tip of my index finger against the tip of my thumb, with the remaining fingers raised, I am making the familiar "Okay" signal. However, I have just unintentionally insulted someone in Brazil!

Generally, I am not the shopper in the family, but one day I went to a familiar retail store to buy a shirt. Approaching the cash register, I noticed the cashier, who was also the department assistant manager, engaged in pages of reports and figures. As she looked up, I proudly handed her my selection. She rang up the purchase, took my money, boxed the shirt and said all the polite things expected at check out. However, we never had eye contact. She remained distracted and focused on her paperwork during our entire exchange. Her words said I was an important customer, but her body language and behavior said the opposite. It was a mixed message. That may seem unimportant, until you consider that I still remember the story and now you know it too.

Unintentional facial expressions also give mixed messages. If Teri comes home excited about a new outfit she bought on sale, I have to be careful not to send a mixed message. My changing expression may hurt her feelings, implying I do not like her outfit. She may worry about my unexpected reaction and eventually return the purchase. This would be unfortunate if my changed expression was actually in response to a ball game on television and not her outfit. In a trusting relationship, it is important to check out these mixed messages, instead of perceiving incorrectly and finding yourself unnecessarily in conflict.

DIRECT AND INDIRECT COMMUNICATION

Some people are painfully direct. My favorite example is from the television series *Frasier*[6]. In discussing a recent argument with his girlfriend, Dr. Frasier Crane said, "I offered her an olive branch and she broke it, burned it and spelled out 'No' in the ashes." Wow. That is direct and unmistakable. God also did not mince words when he said repeatedly, "Thou shalt not!" Jesus could be direct also. He said things like: "Judge not, that you be not judged." "Arise take up your pallet and walk." "You shall not tempt the Lord your God." Direct communication leaves little room for interpretation or doubt. When Dad sternly says, "Go to your room," his words do not suggest the alternative of detouring through the kitchen for a snack!

Indirect communication offers more flexibility. Jesus spoke in parables about mustard seed, hidden treasure, pearls and prodigals. Books and sermons have been written through the centuries offering unique and innovative interpretations of what he meant. He also said, *"If any one thirst, let him come to me and drink."* However he was referring to spiritually charged, living waters, not Evian or Perrier. What does Dad mean when he asks, "Do you know what time it is?" He may be implying it is bedtime or asking if homework has been completed. However, he may have misplaced his watch.

Here is how it works. A direct person asking, "Why did you do that?" is generally seeking a cause and effect. He wants to know your design or logic. He is asking why you did *this* and not *that*. An indirect person asking the same question is typically implying a problem exists. She is asking for a reason or motive. Conflict will likely occur when a direct person, especially a supervisor, parent or pastor asks the same question of an indirect person. The direct person is seeking information, but the indirect person perceives she has done something wrong. This lends itself to defensiveness or unnecessary confrontation.

LISTENING

I believe one of the greatest compliments you can give someone is to listen to what they have to say without judging, criticizing or predicting their next word. Listening is not the same as agreeing, but it is an effective tool for avoiding miscommunications and resolving interpersonal conflict.

However, sometimes listening is not hearing. It is simply being in the same room, while reading the newspaper, watching television or eating breakfast. Sometimes ineffective listening involves hearing sounds, but not actual words! Sometimes the listener gets the gist of the speaker's perspective and immediately jumps in with his response. Sometimes we have unintentional emotionally deaf moments.

One day during lunch, Teri told me about a note she had written to my mother. She mentioned running by the Post Office to buy stamps and reminded me I needed to call my mother later to thank her for a recent gift. However as Teri was speaking, I experienced an emotionally deaf moment. Her story reminded me of a letter I needed to complete and have signed immediately by my Director. I had forgotten he would leave the office that afternoon for several days and time was of the essence. Teri's story had created anxiety over the forgotten letter, causing me not to hear most of what she had to say.

An emotionally deaf moment is not the same as being distracted by television or computer games. It occurs when something in the conversation causes you to have an emotional response, drawing your thoughts away from the speaker and into your personal conflict. Unless you have a trusting relationship with the speaker, these incidents may easily create more conflict by implying a lack of interest.

Listening is an important skill while trying to resolve conflict. It takes time and patience, but has the potential to build on a foundation of trust. Here are three tips to remember.

1. *You can't listen while talking.* Take a breath! Slow down and let the other person talk. Unless you remain quiet and attentive, you cannot fully understand what the speaker is saying. If your primary intent is to get your point across or win the argument, instead of listening, you will seldom resolve your differences or reach common ground. Proverbs instructs, *he who restrains his words has knowledge* (Prov.17:27).

2. *Remain objective.* Listening and understanding do not imply agreement. The speaker is entitled to voice an opinion, even if it is biased, illogical or imbecilic. You may be surprised to stumble into brief moments of agreement along the way, making the trip worthwhile. Proverbs instructs, *an intelligent mind acquires knowledge, and the ear of the wise seeks knowledge* (Prov.18:15)

and *the purpose of a man's heart is like deep water, but a man of understanding will draw it out* (Prov. 20:5).

3. *Respond to the message and not the messenger.* If my daughter says she wrecked the car and I react emotionally over the damage, without allowing her to explain what happened or asking if she was hurt, I may be perceived as discounting her safety. If your employee expresses a horrible idea, do not make it personal. If you patiently explain why the idea will not work, he may bring you a great idea next week. If you laugh and call him a loser, he may keep his great idea to himself. Why deprive yourself? Proverbs again instructs, *good sense makes a man slow to anger* (Prov.19:11).

SUMMARY

Most of us do not communicate as effectively as we think! My younger daughter, Megan, proved this to me many years ago. The family was seated around the kitchen table enjoying a meal of vegetable soup and cornbread. I noticed two-year-old Megan, in her high-chair, having an unusually good time. She had discovered that by reaching deeply into her soup bowl, she could color most of her arm an appetizing shade of orange. She could also pick out small pieces of vegetable that she liked, while leaving the rest drifting in a murky pool of soaked crackers.

Wanting to be a good parent, I said, "Megan, please use your spoon." She looked up only instantly and hardly slowed down. She obediently picked up her spoon, held it tightly in her left hand, and continued sorting through her bowl with her right hand[7]. Our hungry little two-year-old proved it is best never to assume effective communication. Always check it out.

Communication brings the potential to resolve conflict or to complicate it beyond belief! Develop your skills wisely. Pay close attention to words or phrases that can be toxic to conflict, such as "I don't care" or telling someone "You don't care." Realistically, you cannot hear his thoughts or know his heart. Remember that about ninety-three percent of all communication is non-verbal and must be interpreted by the recipient. You simply cannot *not* communicate. Huh?

TWELVE

ATTITUDES

Several trainees gathered around a table in the Break Room. It was their first month in a new office. They were still learning names and faces, so they preferred to take breaks and go to lunch together. Their conversation was interrupted as Glenda came in to fill her coffee mug. It was one of those huge 24-ounce mugs that should provide enough caffeine to keep her buzzing for several hours. Coffee was fifty cents a cup, but as Glenda dropped her two quarters into the box, she laughed and said, "Well, they don't say what size cup." The trainees rolled their eyes and returned to their conversation.

Before leaving, Glenda stopped at the table to be sociable. She admitted having heard their conversation about one of the trainees wearing a new outfit. She said, "That's such a pretty new outfit. The color goes so well with your eyes. They're just doing great things with plus sized outfits now." Glenda departed, leaving the group in disbelief.

Glenda's attitude likely expands beyond the boundaries of taking advantage of the office coffee fund or making impolite comments. Chances are most people in the office rarely do or say anything to address Glenda's behavior. The tendency in most offices, churches or social clubs is to say "Oh, that's just Glenda."

Everybody has an attitude to some degree. The very good ones and the very bad ones are easiest to spot. A person with a good attitude brings the potential for harmony and resolution to almost any disagreement. However, negative *Attitudes* can bring serious complications.

The Book of Nehemiah offers an interesting perspective on bad attitudes. It is found neatly tucked away in those pages of your Bible which likely remain crisp and seldom read.

The Southern Kingdom of Israel was obliterated by the Babylonians in 587 BC. About fifty years later, the Persians overthrew the Babylonians and released all of the exiled Israelites. Slowly, the Israelites began filtering back into their homeland to start the arduous process of rebuilding.

Nehemiah, a wine steward for the King of Persia, convinced the king to allow him to go back home to repair the land where his ancestors were buried. At home in Judea, he found the city walls broken and the gates burned. The task was to rebuild the temple, the city walls and ultimately to awaken and rebuild the people's hope.

However it seldom fails, as soon as you get a new project off the ground or start feeling good about yourself, some self-proclaimed expert on matters of life and relationships intrudes with something like, "Do you mind if I'm perfectly honest?" or "I know it's none of my business, but...." Suddenly, interpersonal conflict intrudes into your sense of well-being.

As the Judeans rebuilt their walls, hope was not the only perspective being circulated. Nehemiah had three antagonists with abrasive attitudes: Sanballat, Tobiah and Gesham. Sanballat, a Samaritan, probably had the worst attitude about the rebuilding campaign. He didn't like the Judeans. His father didn't like the Judeans. His grandfather didn't like the Judeans. You get the idea! So, he had nothing good to say about the ambitious campaign.

Sanballat said things like: "What are these feeble Jews doing? This sounds like a good idea, but they won't make the necessary sacrifices. Do they think they can just wrap up this project in a day? This kind of job will take years! Can they transform burned discarded stones into building blocks for a great temple?" Tobiah chimed in with "Look at what they are building. If a fox jumps up on the wall he could break it down." Maybe this is where we get the idea of a big bad wolf huffing and puffing and blowing down houses.

These attitudes are still not unusual. Bad attitudes criticize the prospects of change and personal development. Bad attitudes mock accomplishments and sow seeds of discontentment, insecurity and self-doubt. However I was once reminded, "A man is never weaker than when he allows himself to be upset by the words of a fool."

Sanballat's words appear to be mocking God and the hard working Judean's, but they also cut deeply into Nehemiah's insecurities. He gave the outward appearance of a bold dynamic leader. On the inside, Nehemiah wondered "Do I have what it takes to coordinate such a massive undertaking? How can I help these people see the wall is *already* half built, while others complain that the wall is *only* half built?" Nehemiah faced an ancient version of the half-full, half-empty cup scenario. He also had to fend off Sanballat and Tobiah's criticisms with something more dynamic than, "Oh Yeah!"

Bad attitudes often have more to do with learned behavior than the person inside. Sometimes they reflect a biased frame of reference. Sanballat was a Samaritan and likely echoing the same racial biases heard from his father and grandfather.

Adversarial attitudes also indicate unsettled emotions and internal conflict. In a hospital clinic waiting room, a young boy was playing with a toy at the feet of his mother. The nurse came to the door and called for his mother. She told her son to stay and play with his toy because she would only be a few minutes. He seemed frozen as she disappeared behind the door. A scowl came to his face as he looked around the room and declared, "I hate my Mommy!"

A few minutes later, as predicted, his mother returned from behind the closed door. The little boy jumped to his feet and ran with a big smile to hug her. The attitude that sounded like anger was actually a frightened, insecure little boy who needed his mother. You'd be surprised how many of those guys are still out there. They are just harder to spot because they are wearing three piece suits, riding motorcycles and making six figure salaries.

The key to handling bad attitudes remains in controlling the part of the interaction you are able to control. Imagine you are driving down a familiar busy street and you approach an intersection. Suddenly a guy in a Hummer (or any massive SUV) cuts you off! You slam on your breaks, blow your horn, then raise your hands in the customary "What are you doing?" pose.

You know the drill. He looks into his rear view mirror. You make eye contact. He lowers his window, sticks out a big burly arm, with an adult hand gesture attached. Now, you are in conflict! You blow your horn again to express your dissatisfaction over his impolite behavior. If you are really feisty, you return the adult hand gesture. But what is the point in all of this?

Let's look at the situation. He cut you off, which was rude, insensitive, and disobedient of the traffic laws. You blew your horn and raised your arms in the customary fashion, indicating your disapproval of his impolite behavior. He insulted you. You insulted him. Now, you are both back in the sixth grade, just driving heavy, high speed vehicles.

When you blew your horn and raised your arms, what did you expect to happen? Think about it. Did you really have no idea he might stick an adult hand gesture out the window?

When he retaliated, which you had to know he would do (He is driving a Hummer!), he just made you more frustrated. Your muscles tensed, your blood pressure increased, but there was little you could do, without getting arrested!

What have we learned about bad attitudes? The guy in the Hummer took an action. Your behavior demonstrated the belief that if you blasted him with your horn he would genuinely appreciate the effort, becoming a more careful driver. WHAT???

You see, the reaction to the bad attitude in this situation resulted in escalated emotions. In this scenario, the only thing controlled by the second driver was his own behavior, which he did not control. His emotional reaction caused an emotional reaction from the Hummer driver and the situation could have become needlessly violent.

When gauging our reaction to an emotional situation or a bad attitude, it is important to have self-awareness. How do I feel? Am I already upset over something else, such as a problem at work or the congested traffic? Am I feeling sad, lonely, unappreciated, frustrated? Did I oversleep, leaving me cranky or short-tempered? Am I running late? Have I had twelve cups of coffee today? Before I can separate the person from the behavior in a conflict situation, I have to understand what is going on with me. Once I can understand and control me, I can more effectively respond to a difficult situation.

It is not effective conflict resolution to ignore bad attitudes. If people continue to say, "Oh, that's just Glenda," she may continue to insult new employees and make life miserable for her co-workers. She may also never develop any self awareness or realize what others think of her.

When Glenda paid the trainee a left-handed compliment, she could have responded, "Thank you for noticing my outfit, but I don't feel your compliment was very sincere. It really hurt my feelings." Glenda may not have anything else to say or may have a sarcastic retort. The point is not to accommodate her bad attitude. Try to address the behavior (the comment hurt your feelings), without attacking Glenda.

Sometimes bad attitudes are used as a means of keeping people at a distance. Thoughts like, "I've been hurt too many times before" build walls to keep out new relationships. Sometimes we fuel them with deep resentments or concealed emotions. I once found a church member's behavior made me very uneasy. She referred to my sermons as "little talks" and seemed unmoved by my efforts to become friends. I could not understand what I had done to warrant such coldness. It took a few years before an emotional conversation with her husband exposed many deep, painful secrets. For this reason, it is important not to take this behavior too personally. The person behind the attitude may be very fragile or psychologically injured.

Bad attitudes seldom have much to do with the person assaulted by their antagonistic behavior. We are usually innocent bystanders. Keep in mind that you did not break this person and likely cannot fix her. She will probably not allow you inside. Try to keep an emotional distance, addressing words and behavior, but not the person. Most importantly, do not expect immediate change. It took a long time to get them to this point. It will take more time for them to develop meaningful self-awareness and heal.

THIRTEEN

EVEN CHRISTIANS GET ANGRY

Do you get angry? Good little boys and girls don't get angry! We are taught to be nice, friendly, accommodating, polite, but never angry. If you raised your voice in anger to a parent, you probably heard, "Don't talk that way to me!" and were sent to your room. If you slammed the door, pouted, fought on the playground, or used curse words, you were told your behavior was unacceptable and likely punished. If your parents believed anger was a sin or unacceptable behavior, it likely met various degrees of punishment such as, bed without dinner, grounded without television, an unreasonable curfew, the belt, switch, paddle or some other weapon of choice!

Since good little boys and girls do not get angry, we efficiently fill our personal lexicon with acceptable words. Instead of angry, we are agitated, stressed, frustrated, perturbed, upset, annoyed, troubled, challenged, irritated, aggravated, or hot n' bothered. However, these euphemisms cannot change the fact that even good Christians get angry. God created us this way. It is an emotion. It is neither good nor bad, until it results in inappropriate or sinful behavior.

Sometimes we forget Jesus also had days when his emotions flared. His confrontation with the Pharisees, while healing a man with a withered hand on the Sabbath (Mark 3:1-6), is the only place where the Bible describes him as *angry*. The original Greek text uses the word *orge* (3:5) to describe Jesus' emotion. This word is most commonly used in the New Testament for *anger* and has no other appropriate translation. Who but the Pharisees could have provoked such a response?

Another familiar example of Jesus' anger erupts from the vivid imagery in John 2:13-16. Jesus' arrival at the temple was met with the sounds of oxen, sheep, fluttering pigeons and the clinking of silver. The money-changers had set up shop in the temple and were making a profit from pilgrims, intending only to worship. With a whip of cords and an explosion of anger, Jesus shouted, overturned tables and drove out the buyers and sellers. We do not know if Jesus actually struck anyone with his whip, but he certainly created a stir! The resulting logic implies either Jesus was sinful or anger is not a sin. I believe anger is a natural human response when someone's personal values are contested or threatened. Of course, there is the *Wrath of God* issue in the Old Testament, but that's not quite the same thing.

This is not to say the Bible condones random and unprovoked anger. A few examples of the Bible's wisdom related to anger include:

> *A man of quick temper acts foolishly, but a man of discretion is patient (Prov. 14:17).*

> *He who is slow to anger has great understanding, but he who has a hasty temper exalts folly (Prov. 14:29).*

> *Be not quick to anger, for anger lodges in the bosom of fools (Eccl. 7:9).*

> *But I say to you, that everyone who is angry with his brother shall be liable in judgment; whoever insults his brother shall be liable to the council, and whoever says, 'You fool!' shall be liable to the hell of fire (Matt. 5:21-22).*

A careful study of these and other related passages implies not a prohibition against anger, but the instruction to be very careful with it. These verses teach preventing sinful behavior. They encourage patience and the resolution of anger, instead of living under the dark shroud of a grudge. Paul writes in Ephesians, *Be angry, but do not let the sun go down on your anger* (4:26).

WHAT IS ANGER?

One of the best explanations of anger, short of a psychological textbook, came from Andrew D. Lester, a former professor at the Southern Baptist Theological Seminary and author of *Coping with Your Anger: A Christian Guide (The Westminster Press, 1983)*. Dr. Lester insightfully describes anger as a response to a threat. Among many other things, this perceived threat may be directed towards your beliefs, values, opinions, family, belongings, self-esteem or physical well-being.

What kinds of things threaten you: aggressive car salesmen, speaking in public, wearing a bathing suit, conservative or liberal politicians, evolution or creationism, or things that go bump in the night? As we mature and our priorities, beliefs and values change, so will those things which we perceive to threaten and invoke our anger.

Imagine it is 3:00am and you have been asleep for hours. Suddenly the crashing of glass snatches you from your dreams. Disturbing movements in the kitchen pull you from the covers to get your Louisville Slugger from under the bed. You stub your toe while putting on your housecoat, but stifle any sound that might signal the intruder. Carefully, you slip through the perilous darkness towards the kitchen. A small night-light is on, but you see no movement. Your body is in attack mode. Your blood pressure is raised; breathing is shallow; your heart is racing; your palms are sweating; your knuckles are white as you tightly grip the baseball bat. A threat is perceived and you are ready!

Upon arrival at the kitchen door, you still hear only slight noises and see no discernable movement in the darkened room. You take a deep breath, switch on the lights with your elbow and raise the baseball bat. You enter the room shouting "Remember the Alamo!" or something equally dramatic. Your threat is not an intruder. It's only Sparky.

Your gray, longhaired, perpetually hungry cat has climbed on the counter to help herself to a snack. While enjoying the late night cuisine, she knocked a glass from the counter with her tail. Your natural response would be to gather sweet Sparky into your arms, telling her what a good kitty she has been. Of course not! Your natural response is to send Sparky scurrying out of the room, seeking shelter under the couch or the nearest chair.

The perceived threat in this situation had blended anger, fear and anxiety. The emotional and chemical reactions transitioned your body into *attack* mode. The intensity was contained until you confronted the threat. However, once you discovered the threat was only Sparky, the stored emotions still had to go somewhere! Instantly, they transformed into anger and launched across the kitchen counter, sending Sparky into hiding.

Anger tends to be complicated. A good way to understand anger is through self awareness. Anger is a good indicator of our priorities. We get angry when important things and ideas are threatened. Many years ago, my preschool age daughter Kirsti found my Bible lying on the coffee table. It seemed a good place to jot a few illegible preschool notes from the morning's sermon. My reaction was a sharp expression of disapproval. That Bible had gone through seminary with me. I used it daily for study and prayer. How dare she use its pages for arts and crafts! She had threatened the sanctity of this intimately prized possession.

Twenty years later, when I turn to those same pages, they have become tear-stained. I am drawn back in time, with different emotions, to a playful little girl who had seen her daddy write in that book many times. She just wanted to be like him.

Anger is a vital part of human nature. It protects us when we are threatened. It also motivates change, uncovers hidden or suppressed emotions and can stir a teenager to take bold strides towards self-determination. Anger can take many shapes. It can be internalized, aggressive, passive-aggressive or assertive anger.

INTERNALIZED ANGER

I have heard it said that anger turned inward is depression and anger turned sideways is sarcasm. When anger is internalized or kept bottled up, it tends to seep into those darkened places of the mind where you prefer not to visit. Anger tends to frighten some people. They would rather it just go away. When it refuses to go away, they try to ignore it. They smile, tell a joke, or eat another candy bar.

When guilt and anger at one's self are forced down into a deepening pool of tears, it tends to transform into shame. I can forgive you if you sin against me. A judge can absolve you of your guilt, but only God can take away your shame! Shame is an internalized anger at the soul.

While in seminary, I pastored a little church on the distant outskirts of Louisville, Kentucky. It was not unusual to receive visitors from the nearby interstate highway requesting money for gas or food. Consequently, the late night knock on my door was not unexpected.

As I opened the door, the light from a nearby telephone pole silhouetted a large man. He appeared wild-eyed and agitated, approximately fifty-five years old, well over six feet tall and considerably over two hundred and fifty pounds. The smell of alcohol drifted with his words. "You the pastor?" I nodded and said I was. "You and I gotta talk. Right now." After visually checking for knives, guns and other dangerous hardware, I invited him inside and led him to the chair in front of my desk. Usually, I sat adjacent to the individual I counseled, but in this instance I found the desk provided reasonable security.

The strange man told me he had seen God. Following that declaration, he just sat staring at me with wild, penetrating eyes. Obviously, he expected a reply! Not knowing what else to say, I asked, "Well, what did he say?" The man shifted to the edge of his chair and took a deep breath, still staring intensely. In words soaked in alcohol, he answered, "God said I gotta get right! That's why I'm here."

Of course he had been drinking. He most likely drank every night. Apparently, he carried the immeasurable weight of internalized anger from many troubled years on those broad shoulders. The night usually made the memories return and the alcohol conveniently silenced them. That night, for some unknown reason, it had not.

The man told me he had seen a snake coiled at the foot of his back steps. Now, it is important to keep this in perspective. He lived deep in the woods. He saw as many snakes in a day as I saw traffic lights. Normally, he would have hit the snake with a shovel or picked it up and bit off its head! Instead, this particular snake had led him onto hallowed ground. Like Moses staring into the burning bush on Mt. Horeb, this man believed he had seen God. He said he wanted to be rid of the guilt, the anger, and the shame. He asked me to baptize him.

He was the tallest, heaviest, most intimidating person I had baptized in my young career. It was all I could do to get him in and out of the water without drowning both of us! Most members kept a reasonable distance, but he became increasingly sociable. More importantly, the guilt and anger were gone. So was the alcohol. Even more amazing than my late night encounter was seeing him in worship each Sunday. Sitting on the back row, mouthing words to hymns he did not know, he was proudly praising the Lord he had met in his backyard.

AGGRESSIVE ANGER

Aggressive anger is when your co-worker comes into your cubical, calls you an obscenity, then picks up your favorite coffee mug and smashes it! The disciple Peter demonstrated aggressive anger when he drew his sword in the Garden of Gethsemane and cut off the Roman soldier's ear as he approached Jesus.

Following a bad review from the judges on the hit television show *American Idol*[8], it is not unusual to see contestants perceiving a threat to their self esteem, storming from the audition room shouting expletives. Aggressive drivers endanger our highways and cause needless accidents. Aggressive anger is often the weapon of choice for those who are insensitive or fail to recognize how their unbridled emotions affect others. It is also used by those who feel hopeless or helpless and find no other alternative.

PASSIVE-AGGRESSIVE ANGER

Anger is not always about slamming doors, screaming obscenities, breaking dishes or pounding fists into walls. Passive-Aggressive anger occurs when that same co-worker comes into your cubicle, compliments you on how well your make-up is covering that horrible zit and *accidentally* knocks your favorite coffee mug to the floor.

Passive-Aggressive anger is more socially acceptable than aggressive anger because it seems less harmful. It is anger in the disguise of things like sarcasm or left-handed compliments, gossip, pouting, silence, over- or under- eating, condescension, forgetfulness and avoidance.

Charlotte is an administrative assistant in a small company. She greets customers, handles incoming telephone calls, orders supplies, and schedules sales appointments. Charlotte believes anger is a sin and refuses to acknowledge she ever becomes angry. However, she does not have the best relationship with one of the salesmen.

Ernie is middle-aged and a flamboyant dresser. He talks on the phone profusely to vendors, co-workers, almost anyone who will listen and many who do not. He is a great salesman, but Charlotte considers him rude, loud and pushy.

Each morning, when Ernie comes through the door he calls "Morning! Who loves you Baby?" Charlotte gives a bright, cheerful response, but prefers to hide under her desk. Some days she dashes into the supply room or restroom when she sees him leave his car.

One day, Ernie stopped at Charlotte's desk. He placed both palms on her desk and leaned towards her. She almost choked from the combination of smoker's breath and pungent cologne. He said, "Darlin' I need your help. I've got an important presentation coming up in two weeks, but I'm going out of town today. I need you to order these supplies for me." He handed her the list and left with, "Darlin', I'm depending on you. Don't let me down."

Charlotte smiled and took the list. She placed it neatly on a stack of requisitions. As days went by, other requisitions made their way on top of Ernie's list. Distractions delayed placing the order. Eventually, Ernie dropped by on the day before his presentation to pick up the supplies. Charlotte had ordered them, but too late. They had not yet arrived. Charlotte apologized and said the right things to appear contrite in her absent-mindedness. However, her passive-aggressive anger had put Ernie at a disadvantage. She got him!

When a wife, such as Kathy, constantly nags Bill to pick up his clothes, knock the mud from his shoes, put his dishes in the dishwasher and wipe away the toast sweat, it may indicate she feels helpless to change his behavior any other way. Frustrated parents do the same thing. The passive-aggressive message is if you loved me, you would do these things because they are important to me. However, that message may not ever be heard. As soon as Kathy opens her mouth, Bill tunes her out. He's heard it all a thousand times. Of course, that is passive-aggressive too!

Passive-aggressive anger can be as unassuming as being *tired* when your wife asks you to clean out the garage, while she goes shopping with the girls. It can be as passive as seemingly *not hearing* your spouse say "I love you" after an argument. However, it carries an aggressive underlying message that says, "I'm still angry and this isn't over."

ASSERTIVE ANGER

Assertive anger is when your co-worker comes into your cubicle and uses non-threatening, non-blaming messages to communicate her anger. She may say something like, "I felt angry (or select euphemism of choice) when you told the boss I was the reason your report was late. Next time you need my help, please give me some specific instructions so I will know what you need and when you need it." This time she makes no reference to your coffee mug.

Jesus demonstrated assertive anger when he confronted the Pharisees while healing a man with the withered hand (Mark 3:1-5). He used logic to defy their righteous indignation. He asked, *"Is it lawful on the Sabbath to do good or to do harm, to save life or to kill?"* The Pharisees were silent as Jesus looked around in anger. He grieved at their hardness of heart and exposed their spiritual perspective as shallow and cold. However, unable to confront Jesus, the Pharisees passive-aggressively went out and conspired against him.

HOW TO MANAGE ANGER

When effectively channeled, anger serves as a great resource when you need to defend yourself in a darkened parking lot. However, it can also be a volatile, disruptive emotion with the power to damage relationships permanently. Unresolved anger carries the potential to alienate family members, shatter the bonds of marriage and corrupt our Christian message of reconciliation. Unless we devise a strategy for controlling anger, rest assured anger will control us.

Beware of the Danger Signs

If good little boys and girls cannot get angry, how does this rule apply to pastors and ministers? Pastors cannot show anger, except as permitted in highly demonstrative sermons. They also cannot curse, argue or openly complain about their congregation, but they still get angry. This is a fact!

The signs of anger may be physical or psychological. Sometimes we deflect it with clichés such as "I just got up on the wrong side of the bed" or "I'm down in the dumps." Some pastors express their anger in more subtle ways. I knew a minister who used food as his substitution for anger. When he became angry, he ate...and ate. He could eat more fried chicken, macaroni and cheese and sheet cake than anyone I knew. Outwardly, he appeared jovial and gracious. Inwardly, he needed to fill a broken, angry heart.

After several weeks of counseling, he finally gave himself permission to care for himself. He began to explore his thoughts, feelings and especially his behavior. He noticed he began snacking when he became angry. When he *grazed* or returned repeatedly to the refrigerator, he stopped and asked himself, "Am I angry? Why?" As he discovered the sources of his anger, he began to find solutions. He also went for brisk walks to diffuse some of the stored emotions. He slowly controlled the anger that had previously controlled him. He also lost seventy pounds.

Take Time Out

At times, my daughter Kirsti could have been the poster child for the *Terrible Twos* or the *Troublesome Threes*. When she broke the rules or had an emotional tirade, the harshest punishment we could issue was *time out*. She would be charged with sitting on a stool or small chair for what seemed to her like an eternity. Actually, it was about ten minutes.

This is an effective tool for adults as well. Once anger is identified and emotions begin to build, the potential for doing or saying something regrettable is high. The solution is to break the emotional cycle: *Time Out*. This is also a good tip for parents with combative children and supervisors with temperamental employees. It can be a brisk walk around the office or down the block. It can be reading unrelated emails, drinking a cup of tea or calling a friend to vent (It's important to get permission first). This is also an excellent method of breaking the cycle of conflict, which will be discussed later.

Be Honest With Yourself and God

While nailed to the cross, Jesus prayed, "My God, my God, why hast thou forsaken me?" and "Into thy hands I commit my spirit." One prayer expressed the raw emotions of a man who had been brutalized, mocked and abandoned by his dearest friends. The other reached into the heavens as a profound declaration of faith. Seemingly, they were prayed only moments apart.

The great cohesive bond in any relationship is trust. Jesus trusted God to love him despite his emotional outburst. He trusted God to love him even when he challenged the nature of their relationship. That level of honesty is essential to resolving deep anger in relationships. Jesus was not afraid of his emotions, nor was he afraid of the God who loved him.

I may prefer euphemisms such as frustration, irritation, or aggravation, but it is anger all the same! I cannot confront my anger until I own it and understand it. Once I identify and confront my anger, I am more self-aware and aware of how my emotions affect others. I am ready to plan a response instead of blurting out a reaction I may soon regret!

Anger complicates any conflict. It makes it more intense and harder to resolve. As in most situations, I usually have more control over *my* anger than anyone else's. Therefore, the conflict resolution should begin there. *Be angry, but do not sin; do not let the sun go down on your anger, and give no opportunity to the devil* (Eph 4:25-27).

FOURTEEN

SOMETIMES SOLUTIONS
ARE OUTSIDE THE BOAT

Many years ago when my daughters were young, I took them to a nearby playground. I saw a little girl about ten years old swinging contentedly, until an older boy ran up from behind and pushed her swing very high. The swing lurched upward and the little girl screamed, tightly clutching the swing chains in her tiny little hands. She began crying as two other children ran to her aide and stopped the swing. The young culprit and his friends stood to the side laughing and pointing. For him the prank was over. However, the precious little face once frozen with fear, now burned with rage. The little girl jumped from her swing, picked up a plastic baseball bat and smacked him across the back of the head. It took a little longer for her to feel the conflict was completely resolved.

A critical dynamic in resolving interpersonal conflict is recognizing when the conflict is resolved for everybody. That is not always an easy thing to do. Notice how differing perspectives lay the foundation for conflict.

SEVENTEEN-YEAR-OLD BECKY: Hi Dad. I'm going to drive Sarah and Ashley to the lake on Saturday. Sarah's dad is going to take us out on his boat after his fishing trip.

DAD: Oh, I wish you had said something sooner. I'd rather you didn't drive this weekend. I need to replace the tires on your car before you make a trip like that.

BECKY: They're depending on me! Sarah's leg is in a cast and Ashley can't drive again until she makes a better grade in Geometry. You're going to ruin everything!

DAD: I'm sorry, but your car isn't safe enough for you guys to drive that far. They're forecasting afternoon thunderstorms.

BECKY: You don't care if I ever have any fun. You just want me to sit home and be miserable. You never let me do anything!

Disappointed Becky's attitude is rather typical and very narrow in perspective. Her priority is to enjoy a weekend at the lake with her friends, not tires or automotive safety. She also has no prior experience with accidents on wet rural highways caused by slippery tires. She is young with no references to warn her of probable hazards. She hears her dad's response only as it affects her social calendar

Dad's detractions and delays have caused him to be the bad guy, but he knows it might rain and the tires need replacing. He also knows Becky is a good, but inexperienced driver. He loves his daughter, but he knows accidents happen when slick tires, inexperienced drivers and road hazards come together. He cannot take a chance with Becky's safety.

It started as the best of times, but quickly became the worst of times. Dad and Becky have very different perspectives. They need to discuss their thoughts and feelings, with as little emotion as possible. This will be difficult since Becky's side of the argument is loaded with emotion. She thinks she has the most to lose. Dad knows better!

In about twenty minutes, both will have calmed enough for another conversation. If Dad takes the time to listen, Becky will describe the plans they have made. He will hear the excitement in her voice and better understand her emotional reaction. However, since Becky's reaction will likely still be emotional and immature, Dad needs to be the adult, which is not always as easy as it seems. His wisdom in finding a workable solution is critical.

Becky is young and does not realize the potential dangers in driving on wet pavement with slick tires. Of course, she sees the glass half-full. It may not rain at all! Dad knows safety has to trump a social outing. Of course, Dad has several alternatives to consider.

First, he could ignore the entire confrontation and assume everything is resolved. That only works if you are a cold hearted buzzard, with no sensitivity for your daughter's feelings. Eventually, Becky and her request for the car will eventually reappear. Dad will not get off that easily! Avoidance is not a productive solution to this problem.

Second, he could dig in his heels and declare himself Lord of the manor! He might say, "You'll not take the car on Saturday- end of discussion". That may end the discussion, but not the conflict. Becky will feel devalued and bullied. She will feel embarrassed that she cannot drive her friends and emotions will begin to fuel resentment. This is competition. One side will win and the other will lose. Neither will be happy...for a long time.

Third, Dad could prefer to be a friend to Becky instead of her parent. He could elect to accommodate her immature outburst, keeping her happy and popular. This only works if nothing serious happens and Dad sees no value in maintaining parental authority. This type of solution accomplishes very little beyond appeasement.

Fourth, Dad can sit down and talk with Becky. He can explain his concern for her welfare and for Ashley and Sarah. He can listen to her side and see if they can find a solution together that allows her to go to the lake, while avoiding a hazardous driving situation. If she briefly looks beyond her disappointment, she may realize her dad is not trying to ruin her weekend. He only has her safety in mind. This brief dialogue, if handled respectfully and calmly will lead to alternatives beyond a simple Yes or No.

A reasonable solution might be for Becky to drive Mom's car to the lake, allowing Dad to replace the slick tires. He might also drive Mom to the hair dresser and grocery as penance for not replacing the tires sooner!

This experience may also enrich Dad and Becky's relationship. Dad may better understand Becky's emotional reaction and need for independence. Becky may take a greater ownership of car maintenance. Realistically, Dad can be pleased if she realizes he's not the party-pooping ogre she once thought. Sometimes the answer is discovered, once we allow ourselves to look for it.

One night, Jesus invited Simon Peter to step out of his fishing boat and into the water for a little stroll (Matthew 14:22-36). Not unlike Becky, Peter's frame of reference was limited. Walking on water was reserved for those with a very unique perspective on faith ... and physics!

As a fisherman, spending the better part of every day on the water, Peter knew beyond fear of contradiction he could not walk on water. He had a pair of soggy sandals drying on his back porch to prove it. However, Jesus offered an alternative Peter had never considered. He walked on the water.

Jesus demonstrated a unique relationship with God that opened new possibilities. You have heard it said we sometimes need to think outside the box to find unusual or non-traditional solutions. Jesus offered Peter a solution *outside the boat*!

It's not always easy to recognize every available solution, especially when we are engaged in conflict. Tempers flare and we tend to get tunnel vision, seeing circumstances and people from narrowing perspectives. The more emotional the situation, the narrower our perspective grows. However if we allow ourselves to hear, consider and even validate different viewpoints, we potentially gain a broader perspective. We don't have to agree with them just to consider them. However by doing so, we open ourselves to possibilities and solutions beyond our personal understanding. If the obvious alternatives do not work, try considering the improbable. What if a man really could walk on the water?

Annie and Karl have been engaged for only a few months, but they have been a couple since high school. Karl recently graduated from college, while Annie still has another year to go. They plan to get married after she graduates, but nothing is carved in stone.

Unexpectedly, Karl received a scholarship to begin an internship hundreds of miles away in Chicago. The news came as excitement, laced with apprehension. The offer could not be reasonably refused, yet they would be separated for at least a year. Would their love survive the test of time and distance? It was the best of times. It was the worst of times.

Almost without notice, Annie began churning with unexpected emotions. Excitement transformed quickly into insecurity. She cried and became distant. She angrily attacked Karl for accepting the new opportunity. She became bitter. She complained that he did not love her and was running away. She said she hated him! She pulled away even more. She came back. Finally, she agreed to travel with him to visit his prospective home.

The trip was enjoyable. They held hands and laughed. Annie seemed happy and even excited again about the possibilities of change. However, it took only a few hours before Annie emotionally crashed again. She became very agitated. She screamed, cried and refused to listen to Karl's reassurances.

Their return home carried an unexpected twist. Karl, who had been the stabilizing force during this troubling turn of events, began having doubts. Could Annie have been right all along? Their relationship was missing something, but what was it? After days of soul searching and emotional discussions, Karl told Annie he needed time alone to sort through his feelings. He believed he still loved her. What was the solution?

They stayed apart for several long days, avoiding phone calls and text messages. Soon Annie demanded a better explanation. What was missing? How could they mend their relationship, if she didn't know what was wrong? Karl genuinely tried to answer but could not. The solution would not be found in the logical, reasonable or obvious. It would be found outside the boat.

Why had Karl changed? Yelling matches with Annie would not lead them to the answer. His perspectives on the internship and their relationship were woven into a frame of reference he had not yet discovered. He certainly could not yet understand.

Karl was a normal, well-balanced young man. He played a musical instrument in a local band. He enjoyed time alone with his music, but had several close friends. He had been successful in a highly complex field of study. However, his childhood and adolescence included memories of a broken marriage. His parents' relationship was characterized by loud arguments and tears, emotional abuse, infidelity, long separations and ultimately divorce. What he did not realize was how Annie's constant arguing and tears had awakened these old childhood memories. After several weeks, Annie's emotional tirades had broken the wall holding back a heavy pool of tears and emotion.

Karl's perspective had been dramatically altered by the arousal of these bitter childhood memories. The old scripts told him anger leads to arguments. Arguments lead to separation, which leads to infidelity, then more anger, longer separation and divorce. It happened to his parents, whom he dearly loved, and it could happen with Annie. Something wasn't missing. Something had arisen from the ashes of his parent's marriage: the possibility of failure.

Conflict brings different perspectives to the table, which may change with each new set of circumstances. Karl saw a bright future in the exciting internship. The offer made him feel valued and successful. Annie shared his excitement, but soon became insecure and eventually angry about the long separation. Annie's anger triggered an emotionally charged psychological response, which brought Karl into a maze of childhood memories. This brought another layer of perspective to the already troubled relationship.

It may seem Karl and Annie's contrasting viewpoints would destroy their relationship. Annie could only see red! Anger, fear, disillusionment, and insecurities had blinded her from any other perspective. Karl could only see blue. He was drowning in a swirling sea of childhood emotion. He was sad, heartbroken, confused. He loved Annie, but saw her becoming an adversary. Could she really be his life partner?

However other colors were yet to be seen. The alternatives to resolve conflict are always present. They may not be readily apparent and are sometimes smothered by two narrow perspectives. For that reason, it is important not to assume things are true because they seem true. Questions should not always be answered from our personal frame of reference, which may not be objective or even rational. Openness to solutions, limited only by our faith in God, in each other and our imagination, may bring surprising results. What if a man really can walk on water? What if solutions and possibilities, not yet considered, are outside the boat? What would I have missed had I not tried to find them?

Annie and Karl must decide if the search is worth continuing. Their story is a tale of two perspectives, complicated by their youthful frames of reference and fear, disappointment, disillusionment and insecurity. Their best solution will not be found by one giving in to the other. That leads to winning or losing, not resolution. It may also lead to many unhappy years of marriage. Instead, the answer will come from openness, honesty, a constructive dialogue, an intimate search for understanding and a deep abiding trust.

In the Garden of Eden, God said Adam and Eve would die if they ate from the Tree of Knowledge of Good and Evil. Theological presuppositions aside, at that moment, they did not die! Instead, they were driven out of the Garden. In other words, an unexpected alternative was found. The penalty for their actions was defined as death. That was undisputed, except in the serpent's speculations. However, God was greater than his rules! He offered grace instead of justice or revenge. He allowed his creation to mature and develop a little longer.

God also demonstrated priorities beyond his own pride. He seemed unconcerned that the serpent might claim he was right all along since they did not die! Sometimes we let things like that get in our way.

Adam and Eve would never return to the Garden. Their innocence was gone. The bell could not be un-rung. Once a husband tells his wife of an affair, she can't "unhear it" and their world has forever changed. They can never return to the innocence of the Garden, but their conflict may still be resolved. Marital death is not always the best alternative.

If a teenager is arrested for shoplifting, lessons may be learned and fines paid, but innocence is lost and consequences may be long lasting. However, the potential for maturity and insight has been made available and may be achieved with some hard work. It just has to be outside the Garden.

God gave Adam and Eve a new starting point. He still allowed them to be fruitful and multiply, as originally intended, only they would have to work for it! Through God's wisdom an alternative was found for a very bad situation, with potentially horrible consequences. You just never know!

Moses was looking for sheep on Mt. Horeb, but found God in a burning bush. Elijah looked for God in a powerful wind, an earthquake and a fire, but he found Him in a still small voice. Paul was looking for righteousness in the prosecution of Christians, but he found it in a stunning bright light on the road to Damascus. Mary Magdalene had gone to the garden tomb to anoint a body, but she found her Savior! You just never know where answers will be found, so it remains important to keep looking and listening for the unexpected. When God does not answer your prayers as you expect, look around and carefully listen. You may have been expecting something red, while God's color is blue! Don't miss it!

FIFTEEN

THE STRATEGIES

My daughter Kirstin quickly claimed all the rights and privileges of being the first-born. She was the first girl born on my side of the family in generations and stole my heart with a single glance. However, her arrival took me into unchartered waters. Who knew girl stuff buttoned from the wrong side?

Kirsti always had trouble with the word "No." We soon needed a proven strategy to curtail her emotional tirades and strong-willed determination. After consulting several parenting books, we chose the *Count to Three Method* of discipline. Whenever she misbehaved, we gave her a chance to recognize and change her behavior before punishment. We slowly counted: one-two-three. At the count of three, punishment was administered, usually as *Time Out*.

One evening, I overheard Kirsti and her younger sister Megan in their playhouse. They were preschoolers doing the sort of things preschoolers do, but I could tell Kirsti was becoming agitated. I knew it was likely because, in a rare moment of self-determination, Megan had failed to follow Kirsti's rules. However, instead of an emotional outburst of shouts, tears and thrown toys, I heard something completely unexpected. In a stern voice, Kirsti said, "Megan, (pause) One…." At such an early age, my daughter learned she could control her sister, not with physical violence, but with a single word!

This is how we learn the scripts and behavior used in interpersonal conflict. We observe them through our parents or other significant adults and incorporate them into our behavior. If conflict means to strike, our arsenal needs to be stocked and ready for battle. Consequently, we incorporate many ageless and sometimes painfully worn phrases into our conflict resolution lexicon:

> *Don't make me have to stop this car!*
> *Did you hear what I said?*
> *Don't make me have to say that again.*
> *If I've told you once, I've told you a thousand times!*
> *Stop crying or I'll give you a reason to cry!*
> *Don't make me have to separate you!*
> *Because I said so!*
> *Sit there until you eat just one!*
> *Just wait until your daddy gets home!*
> *As long as you live under my roof, you'll live by my rules.*

We tend to fall back on these phrases because of their familiarity. They worked for our parents, suggesting they must be from some insightful inter-generational parenting guide. However, these are not *state of the art* weapons. They rely on absolute power to obliterate conflict, instead of insightfully orchestrating reconciliation. Effectively resolving conflict requires using strategies appropriate for the circumstances.

BETTER STRATEGIES

Five highly recognized conflict resolution strategies are: Avoidance, Competition, Accommodation, Compromise and Collaboration.

Avoidance sounds a lot like sticking your head in the sand or the coward's way out, but it can be an effective strategy. Sometimes patience is needed to acquire additional information or finalize important details. Avoidance may also be effective as a politically correct alternative, such as avoiding a confrontation with your boss, or if the situation is not important enough to warrant the investment of time and energy. Sometimes when emotions are too volatile and proceeding may cause circumstances to worsen, avoidance provides a reasonable alternative.

After learning King Herod had killed John the Baptist, Jesus invited his disciples to come with him to a *lonely* place. It was a hectic time for Jesus and his disciples. They hardly had time to eat and danger awaited their first miss-step. Jesus realized the value of avoiding any other conflict, until he and his disciples were better prepared.

After speaking so candidly of his death at the Last Supper, dismissing Judas to complete his ghoulish transaction and confronting his friend Peter with the unsettling truth about his denials, Jesus withdrew into the deep shadows of Gethsemane. He knew he could be arrested at any moment. He also knew he needed prayer and meditation before he took on anything else. Avoidance of immediate conflict with the Roman authorities gave Jesus an opportunity to prepare for the terrifying ordeal yet to come.

As Jesus stood in judgment, Pilate, the Roman governor, asked, "Are you the King of the Jews?" If Jesus answered, "*Yes,*" he played into the hands of those who wanted to crucify him. He could not truthfully answer "No." In either case, his answer was irrelevant to the outcome, so Jesus chose avoidance, replying, "You have said so." When Pilate asked, "Do you not hear how many things they testify against you?" Jesus refused to answer. However, his silence should not be mistaken for passive aggressive silence. Neither does his response reflect a mind-game intended to frustrate his accuser. It was a calculated strategy used to avoid further complicating his already dangerous circumstances.

Avoidance effectively allows time to break the cycle of conflict or time for assessment. It is also effective when used to side-step unnecessary or potentially volatile conflict. However, it may leave emotional wounds untreated, important issues unresolved and restrict the development of trust when used as a long-term strategy in troubled relationships. It proverbially sweeps disagreements under the rug, promising they will be tripped over later.

Competition is mostly about power. It is a proven strategy of parents, supervisors, teachers, bullies and police officers. It invokes the phrase, "Because I said so!" which implies absolute power. As a conflict resolution strategy, competition creates winners and losers, as in baseball, football or soccer. It is the preferred strategy of children who run to the car shouting "Shotgun," the driver who cuts you off in traffic, and the insecure husband, refusing to allow his wife to go to the grocery store or beauty shop by herself. Competition is also in play when a husband and wife sequester themselves behind closed doors, screaming obscenities and accusations.

When Jesus approached the temple, realizing buyers and sellers had defiled the sacred halls of worship, he elected to compete. He made a whip of cords, overturned tables, poured out coins, drove people away and shouted, "Destroy this place!" He intended to win!

As a strategy, competition creates leaders and followers. It implies a struggle for control, although some control or authority may be already established and necessary. Parents and teachers have responsibilities requiring them to win conflicts with children over judgment and behavior. Police officers cannot avoid confronting criminal activity. They are sworn to use all necessary resources to protect the public. A boss may have a project with a short deadline and several specific, critical requirements. She may not have the luxury of discussing alternatives.

Competition has the potential to create the sensation of absolute power and powerlessness. If a police officer is standing at my car window, with blue lights flashing, and his citation book in hand, I am powerless to change the law or my previous actions. He may allow me some minor influence over his perspective, but even this is under his control.

A boss may claim to prefer a participatory style of management, but if his actions imply it is his way or the highway, competition is at hand. The boss wins, as long he considers resentment, anger, sarcasm, avoidance, or apathy acceptable collateral damage.

Powerlessness feels like disappointment, frustration, helplessness, hopelessness and a broken heart. It breeds emotions like anxiety and depression. Imaginations run wild with speculation and obsessions. Jesus prayed, *"My God, my God, why hast thou forsaken me?"* Realistically, God had not forsaken him, but it felt that way. How easily you and I can feel equally powerless.

Sometimes competition is less intense. Siblings compete for parental attention. Co-workers compete for recognition or a preferred project. Church members compete for the pastor's attention. Sunday school classes even compete for the highest attendance or greatest contribution to the Mission fundraising drive.

Competition has its merits. Competition in industry often brings innovation, improvement and reasonable prices. In sports, it teaches children to lose respectfully and to win gracefully. However, it can also fuel the hostility in parents, sitting in the bleachers, shouting insults at the nearsighted umpire, who made an unfair call against someone's perfect little darling!

As children mature into adolescence and early adulthood, wise parents move beyond competition onto more productive strategies. Churches allowing competition in leadership meetings or business sessions rarely meet the needs of members needing harmony, acceptance and grace.

Jesus said if anyone strikes you on the right cheek, let him strike you on the left. In ancient Judea, the right hand was considered the dominate hand. The left hand was considered impure. Therefore, a strike to your right cheek would have to be made with the back of the right hand. This constituted an insult, not a combative blow to the face. A competitive response would be to return insult for an even greater insult. However, by instructing us to turn the other cheek, Jesus sought not to compete but to demonstrate grace.

Accommodation is another strategy with mixed value. Generally, people-pleasers and those who do not want to make waves employ accommodation daily. If competition is the strategy of choice for stern parents, accommodation is the preferred strategy of ineffective parents or indulgent grandparents. Accommodation tends to placate one side of the conflict, while discounting or delaying the needs or interests of the other. It tends to work best as a temporary strategy.

Sometimes accommodation is useful when you want to build confidence in the other person. The story of the Israelite Judge, Gideon, offers insight into the effective use of accommodation (Judges 6:33-40). God told Gideon to take his army and attack the Midianites and the Amalekites. Apparently, these were fierce adversaries and Gideon suffered from insecurity. He asked God to give him a sign. He placed a fleece on his threshing room floor. If in the morning, the fleece was dry while the floor around it was wet from the dew, he knew God would be on his side. It worked. The next morning the fleece was dry, but the floor was wet with dew.

However, the Amalekites and Midianites had him out numbered and promised to put up a good fight. Gideon needed a little more convincing. He asked God for an encore performance, but with a twist.

This time he asked for the fleece to be wet and the floor dry. Again, it worked. However, the problem with testing God and asking for signs is that you become addicted to signs and tests. If you keep asking for proof, you have very little opportunity to develop your faith.

It Gideon's case, accommodation was a necessary strategy. God needed Gideon to lead his people into battle against the Midianites. Gideon needed a confidence boost and God provided it. Eventually, by accommodating Gideon's need for signs and assurances, God's people prevailed.

Sometimes accommodation is effective when we have very little invested in the outcome. Suppose you find yourself in conflict with a colleague over an issue that is more important to him than you. Why not accommodate his needs, wants or objectives this time, so you have a bargaining chip when an issue arises with more importance?

Accommodation is also appropriate for expressing unconditional love. I was an introverted child, with very few playmates. Generally, I used my imagination to conjure battlefields, ballparks and scenes from the Wild West. I also had an imaginary friend with whom I shared these exciting episodes: Skootle. He appeared one night as a character in one of my grandfather's bedtime stories and made return appearances. Eventually, I incorporated Skootle into my childhood fantasies.

During the summer between First and Second Grade, I accompanied my grandparents during their Florida vacation. We loaded the white Chevrolet and in the era before Interstate highways, DVDs and CD players, drove several hundred miles, for an enjoyable, sunny vacation. However, the return trip proved more memorable than expected.

Anticipating a long, boring drive back to South Carolina, my grandparents decided to give me one final blast at one of Florida's famous recreational gardens. They took me for boat rides and walks through the flowers. They bought ice cream and souvenirs. Finally, I was sunburned, full of carbohydrates and tired. It seemed safe to hit the road.

We settled back into the cramped little car and sped down the highway. Thirty miles later, a scream from the back seat pierced the tranquil drive. My grandfather swerved, then guided the car towards the shoulder. My grandmother peered over the seat. Her frantic look implied I had unintentionally opened the back door and was about to fall. As we slid along the graveled shoulder, she demanded to know what was wrong. I told her, "We left Skootle."

My grandfather, being the more indulgent, asked where we had left him. To this day, I cannot explain what provoked this incident, but I told him we left Skootle in the parking lot. More than a half hour later, we drove back into the near empty parking lot. I opened the door and Skootle, my imaginary friend, got in the car. For whatever reason, other than he loved me and did not want to see me cry, my grandfather drove thirty miles out of his way, to accommodate my perceived loss.

Of course, that story seems incredulous. Why would anyone accommodate a child to such extremes? The answer is simple: love. Fifty years later, this story still brings tears to my eyes and the fond memory of an indulgent grandfather who would rather be inconvenienced than to see my heart broken. Perhaps it also gave me a more intimate understanding of: *For God so loved the world that he gave his only son, that whoever believes in him should not perish but have eternal life.*

Compromise is a strategy suited for acknowledging the needs, objectives, goals and expectations of both sides in a dispute. It is not the preferred strategy of those who intend to win at all cost. It is not a preference of those who do not have the time to invest in listening or searching for areas of compatibility. Compromise takes time, patience, motivation and the development of trust.

Abraham's negotiation with God over the fate of Sodom and Gomorrah is one of the first great examples of compromise. God declared the pervasive sin in the two cities intolerable and vowed to destroy them. Abraham apparently had a soft heart and felt God had acted too harshly. He said, "Suppose there are fifty righteous men hidden somewhere in these corrupt cities. Is it justified to destroy the righteous along with the wicked?" God said, "Okay, I'll take a closer look. If I can find fifty righteous men, I'll spare the whole place."

Abraham had been to Sodom and Gomorrah and feared his offer might stretch the boundaries of possibility. After some thought, he came back to God with a new deal. Suppose you find forty-five? Suppose you find forty? Suppose you find thirty, twenty or ten? Would God destroy ten righteous men along with the wicked? Eventually, only Lot, his wife, two daughters and potential sons-in-law were spared. Of course, Lot's wife broke the rules and still did not make it! Nevertheless, God compromised to allow Abraham time to draw his own conclusions about the wickedness of Sodom and Gomorrah.

God said the time had come to destroy these sinful cities. For whatever reason, Abraham wanted them spared. God agreed if ten righteous men could be found, the cities would be spared, even though he preferred to find forty, fifty or more! If Sodom and Gomorrah had been spared by the terms of the compromise, God and Abraham would have gained, but not much would have been accomplished. The flaw in compromise is that it tends to leave both sides wanting more.

Collaboration is the most mutually acceptable and far-reaching, long-term conflict resolution strategy. It seeks out the goals, objectives, needs, emotions, and expectations of all participants, intending for everyone to win. If compromise takes time, patience, motivation, and trust, collaboration requires even more. Too often, the bottom line in conflict becomes how much damage I can avoid or "I'll show them who is toughest!" However, Jesus took a less selfish approach. He asked how his actions could glorify and fulfill the purpose of God.

In the Garden of Eden, humanity fractured its covenant relationship with God. Since that time, God has been trying to collaborate with us to restore the covenant. When King Solomon dedicated the new temple, God offered very succinct terms:

If my people, who are called by my name humble themselves, and pray and seek my face, and turn from their wicked ways, then I will hear from Heaven, and will forgive their sin and heal their land (2 Chronicles 7:14).

As time passed with little progress, God offered a new covenant. It was another collaborative offer allowing humanity to achieve forgiveness, spiritual wholeness and abundant life, while providing God the worshipful, obedient, committed relationship he had always wanted. Both sides of the covenant would have their goals, objectives and needs met. God said to Jeremiah:

I will put my law within them, and I will write it upon their hearts; and I will be their God, and they shall be my people. And no longer shall each man teach his neighbor and each his brother, saying, 'Know the Lord,' for they shall all know me, from the least of them to the greatest, says the Lord; for I will forgive their iniquity and I will remember their sins no more (Jer. 31:33-34).

Jesus reinforced God's intended collaboration as he spoke to his followers after the resurrection. He told them to go into all the world and make disciples, baptizing them and teaching them to observe the sacred teachings. In return, he promised to be with them always, even until the end of the world.

Sometimes crisis and conflict can make us feel like our world is coming to an end. Sometimes questions cannot be answered or emotions controlled, without an abiding spiritual presence to guide us. The collaborative spirit of God welcomes that relationship. A collaboration in business, school, at home or play establishes a similar mutually beneficial covenant. It may change our perspective from I want a bigger piece of the pie, to I need to savor and share the nourishment I have with those who have not. Jesus gave a simple two-step guide for collaboration:

Love the lord your God with all your heart and with all your soul, and with all your mind. Love your neighbor as you love yourself.

SIXTEEN

A MISUNDERSTOOD STRATEGY

If your brother sins against you, go and tell him his fault, between you and him alone. If he listens to you, you have gained your brother. But if he does not listen, take one or two others along with you, that every charge may be established by the evidence of two or three witnesses. If he refuses to listen to them, tell it to the church. And if he refuses to listen even to the church, let him be to you as a Gentile and a tax collector. Truly, I say to you, whatever you bind on earth shall be bound in heaven, and whatever you loose on earth shall be loosed in heaven. Matthew 18:15-18

The Christian congregation has endured conflict over issues ranging from closed communion, divorce, dancing, drinking and women's ordination, to color schemes, carpet samples, and misappropriation of church funds. In some circles, the quintessential biblical model for resolving these problems is Matthew 18:15-18.

Church members on the early American frontier lived hard and often died young. Liturgy and orthodoxy gave way to hard praying and uncomplicated worship. Itinerant preachers got their parishioners saved and baptized quickly, because you never knew what calamity the next winter or shootout might bring. Matthew 18 served as a well defined, *no questions asked* framework for handling problems. Got an issue with someone? Go speak with him personally. If that does not work, take along a couple of neighbors for the next conversation. If the stubborn culprit remains unrepentant, take him before the church and cite your case. If he remains unrepentant, treat him like an ancient tax collector. Run him out of church on a rail! It was swift, efficient and biblical!

However, I remain unconvinced this was Jesus' preferred strategy. I fear it is a mistake to leave relationships to a single set of hard-coded rules, without the influence of the greater biblical context. In the preceding passage, Jesus warned his disciples not to cause someone to stumble, making it their business to find the sheep that has gone astray. The depth of his concern for the sinner and the abiding relationship is paramount.

The rules established in Matthew 18: 15-18 are intended for general church discipline, such as for the misappropriation of church funds. This passage applies to a sin serious enough to remove a member from the congregation. However, if misapplied to a deeply interpersonal situation, the impact may be spiritually destructive. The right process used for the wrong circumstance is still the wrong process. Consequently, Jesus' words should be applied only with his redemptive, gracious spirit.

The passage begins, *if your brother sins against you go and tell him his fault, between you and him alone. If he listens to you, you have gained your brother.* This lays the foundation for resolving conflict calmly and respectfully. It brings two individuals together, face to face, not over the telephone, email or texting. This is a great strategy!

The misunderstanding usually occurs with the instruction, *but if he does not listen, take one or two others along with you, that every charge may be established by the evidence of two or three witnesses.* This does not imply busing two members of your afternoon bible study group over to Mrs. Johnson's house to witness and intimidate. This will make matters worse.

Suppose Bill accuses Ernest of pocketing money from the offering plate. If no one else witnessed Ernest's alleged theft, does it do any good to have Sam and Barney accompany Bill to hear him accuse Ernest again? This simply escalates the problem by including two other, previously uninvolved church members. No proof is offered, simply an allegation, but the bell has been rung! Sam and Barney cannot pretend they did not hear the allegation.

Sam and Barney will draw conclusions, in part, by their previous perceptions of Ernest. If they believe him to be honest, ethical and forthright, they may consider the allegations meritless. If Sam is already suspicions of Ernest, the accusation may confirm his opinion. However, suppose Barney had a business deal with Ernest, which caused some disadvantage to Barney. Do you suppose he will be predisposed to give Ernest the benefit of the doubt? Circumstances may even worsen as Sam and Barney go home, tell their wives or discuss the matter at the drug store.

Ernest may never be charged with theft. No proof or corroborating evidence may ever be heard. However, what is the likelihood of Ernest serving on the Stewardship Committee or as an usher next year? This irresponsible behavior is not consistent with Jesus' design.

The implication is to include two or more witnesses who have observed the offense and will corroborate the indictment. This is consistent with scripture the disciples should already know:

A single witness shall not suffice against a person for any crime or for any wrong in connection with any offense that he has committed. Only on the evidence of two witnesses or of three witnesses shall a charge be established (Deut 19:15).

Consequently, Jesus expects no less than two or three witnesses to corroborate the accusation, if the conflict is allowed to distance a member from his church home.

Matthew 18:15-18 prescribes a judicial process for banishing an unrepentant member. I am sure these things happen, but as a conflict mediator, I have not seen a legitimate one. I believe Jesus would have forgiven and accepted a repentant sinner, even for the most serious offense.

In many cases, interpersonal conflict involves differences of opinion, personality or priorities. Sometimes it involves garden-variety pettiness and should get as little airtime as possible! It seems more appropriate to apply other, less judicial guides for conflict resolution, also approved by Jesus,

Therefore all things whatsoever ye would that men should do to you, do ye even so to them: for this is the law and the prophets. (Matthew 7:12), or *Thou shalt love the Lord thy*

God with all thy heart, and with all thy soul, and with all thy strength, and with all thy mind; and thy neighbor as thyself (Luke 10:27-28).

While the model in Matthew is more structured, perhaps the story of Jesus and a woman caught in adultery offers a more conciliatory strategy for resolving interpersonal conflict (John 8:1-11). Jesus encountered church leaders at the temple, presumably already at stage two of Matthew's model. The witnesses were assembled in their righteous indignation and boldly accusing the woman.

These church leaders also knew their scripture. That is probably how they became church leaders! They cited passages, likely memorized from Leviticus and Deuteronomy, to justify not just removing her from the temple, but stoning her to death. From the strictly biblical perspective, they were right. Jesus knew it. Scripture was on their side!

Jesus did not challenge their scriptural integrity, which may have made the discussion too personal. They were already looking for a fight, so why make it worse? He suggested they consider how hard it is to be perfect. Jesus did not make excuses or try to defend the woman's sinfulness. He told them to get in line. "Let him who is without sin among you cast the first stone."

Notice how the older, probably more learned church leaders, understood Jesus' insight quicker than the others. As deeply devoted students of scripture, they intimately understood how difficult it is to obey the letter of the Law, especially in matters of the heart.

Only the woman and her accusers know what Jesus wrote in the sand that day. Some say he listed sins committed by her accusers, possibly including a few of their own marital indiscretions. Maybe he was only doodling in the sand, so his message about using the church and scripture for your own selfish reasons could register in their hardened hearts. Possibly, he was allowing time for tempers to cool and perspectives to change.

I knew a deacon who considered divorce intolerable. He declared it a cowardly, distasteful sin. He excused it for adultery, as did Jesus, but otherwise believed it left the offender stained with shame. "Marriage is for life," he said, "Marriage is for better or worse. When marriage gets tough, you tough it out!"

128

Unfortunately, he learned his only daughter and grandchild had suffered verbal and emotional abuse for several years. Saddened by their mistreatment, he helped them relocate, paid legal fees and defended his daughter's divorce as the only viable alternative. Afterwards, he seemed less inclined to cast the first stone.

Finally, only Jesus and the sinner remained on the stage. As shame welled in her tearful, swollen eyes, she must have wondered what would come next. Unexpectedly, Jesus told her he did not condemn her and not to do it again. He gave her another chance. This seems remotely similar to God's response to Adam and Eve's sin in the Garden of Eden.

It is relatively easy to assume your sins are worse than mine. In fact, I can get a little personal satisfaction from that realization. However, Jesus says if I judge others, I open myself to judgment. Jesus' encounter with the adulterous woman offers a better model for interpersonal conflict resolution than Matthew 18:15-18, because it begins with the accuser, instead of the accused.

Before I condemn you, I am required to look at myself. However, Jesus expects more than a casual glance in the mirror. His dramatic pause to scribble in the sand gives me time to look into the crevices of my own sin. He wants me to hear words I have spoken. He invites me to observe my actions and listen to my thoughts during a day at work. He is suggesting that I count the number of sins I commit before lunch each day and to pray for forgiveness, before I cast a stone in your direction.

Interpersonal conflict is difficult. Just when it seems you have the answers, someone changes the questions! If someone sins or creates congregational conflict, it will be easy to invoke Matthew 18 and run the unrepentant scoundrel out of your church in four methodical steps. You can fire him if he threatens the cohesiveness of your business. What about family conflict?

How will you respond if your son or daughter comes home, after curfew, smelling of alcohol? How will you bring resolution and not make matters worse? At what point does a compassionate parent exorcise a conflicted child from the bond of family? If a friend betrays your trust, causing you embarrassment, how will you respond? If you find someone's phone number in your wife's jacket, how will you learn she is actually ordering your birthday present and not having an affair?

Jesus uses several methods for confronting interpersonal conflict in the story of the woman caught in adultery. *First*, when confronted by the Scribes and Pharisees, Jesus did not argue. They were prepared to debate the merits of their case. In similar situations, we tend to become defensive and return fire. Sometimes the best we can muster is a scowl and an intellectually stimulating "Oh Yeah." I think Jesus realized the situation called for a less antagonistic approach.

Second, the situation was already emotional, especially for the accused woman, and Jesus chose not to let it escalate. He could have shouted the hidden sins of the accusers to embarrass them. Instead, he paused, making marks in the sand. He stepped away from the emotion and the accusations to let everyone gather their composure, if only while wondering what he was doing.

Third, he insisted on self-awareness. Let him who is without sin cast the first stone! This is not to say sinlessness or perfection is required before we address problems or administer discipline. However, we are expected to look inwardly before casting the first stone. If I am angry, bitter or jealous, do I understand how it may affect my behavior or judgment? If I condemn someone's behavior, are my motives pure enough not to condemn the person also? If I am critical or intolerant, will I have the insight to understand why?

The woman's accusers did not leave because she was no longer guilty. They left because they were! Their righteous indignation over the woman's sin was only pretentious. They cared very little about her, her husband, her lover or her sin. They were using this woman's indiscretion as a means of attacking Jesus. The sinful, dehumanized woman was collateral damage.

Interpersonal conflict can be about words, ideas, actions or perceptions. It can be about temptations, transgressions or sins. It can be about curtains, carpet, choir robes, church organs or tape recorders. Jesus understood that conflict resolution is ultimately about reconciling people and restoring relationships. Maybe that is why his final step takes us back to the basics. His words remind us that all have sinned and fallen short of the glory of God. But beyond our considerable sins, stands the shadow of an old rugged cross. Let us all go and sin no more!

SEVENTEEN

SAY A LITTLE PRAYER FOR ME

Sometimes conflict is overwhelming and confusing. It often pulls us into uncharted waters, finding us unprepared to step out of our boat and walk. The following is a guide to use whenever conflict pulls you from your comfort zone. The five easy steps can be easily remembered using the word: P-R-AY-E-R.

PAUSE

The first step breaks the cycle of conflict: Pause. When conflict becomes intense or overwhelming, rarely will good things happen if you continue. Suppose an aggressive employee barges into your office or your teenage son bolts from the room after learning he cannot have the car Friday night. Suddenly, your emotions intensify. Your muscles tense. Your heart rate increases. You can no longer think clearly and objectivity quickly fades. Briefly bring the conflict to a halt. Step away from it. Take time-out.

Instead of escalating the argument or shutting down from anxiety, take a break to regain your composure or allow the circumstances to calm. Tell the aggressive employee or your angry son that you would like to continue this conversation, but some time is needed for everyone to put things in perspective. Ask for a chance to talk again in twenty minutes. It is important to be specific. Say something like, "Let's get together at four o'clock" not "We'll talk after dinner."

Thirty minutes seems too long and may make your employee or son feel unimportant or dismissed as a distraction. That is not the intention. Ten minutes does not allow enough time for intense emotions to calm. Twenty minutes generally works.

Use your twenty minutes wisely. It is not the time for another phone call or email. It is time to focus, not pout! Say a brief prayer - or a long one. Use meditation techniques. Go for a brisk walk. Allow yourself and others the opportunity to begin again.

An excellent *Pausing* technique comes from the old adage *count to ten*. If you find yourself becoming inappropriately emotional, instead of counting to ten, recite multiplication tables or calculate mathematical equations. Just start simply: 1+1=2, 2+2=4, 4+4=8, 8+8=16. You get the idea. Then make it a little more complicated as the emotion begins to subside.

The point of this exercise is to transition your mind from emotions or confusion to logic and objectivity. Give yourself and your counterpart opportunity to step away from the conflict long enough to avoid saying or doing something unfortunate. Accept your twenty minutes as a moment of grace.

Remember that introverts may need a little longer to internalize and process everything. Twenty minutes may not be long enough. Sometimes emotions become too volatile or fragile or the conflict is too severe for a twenty minute break to do much good. In these cases, set the time to return to the conversation whenever you perceive it to be most productive. Be sure to set a mutually acceptable time and place for your next conversation. At that time, if you are still not ready, reschedule, but be specific. You may say you will get together tomorrow at three o'clock in the Living Room or at Noon next Friday at the Blue Top Grill. Just remember that comments like, "We'll talk again when you get your head straight" or "Call when you're ready to talk" tend to be counter-productive.

REFLECT

Once the cycle of conflict has been temporarily paused, reflect on what has happened. Begin to understand the *action* and what *beliefs* may be complicating or influencing *behavior*. While this sounds a little technical for someone in a heated conflict that is precisely the point. By engaging in a brief analysis, you begin using a different part of your brain. It serves the same purpose as counting or calculating instead of fuming! Consider the potential *consequences* of the most recent exchange. Actions will have consequences. Is this where you want to go?

ACKNOWLEDGE YOURSELF

Self-awareness is critical when engaging conflict resolution. Acknowledge yourself by considering how your perspective or emotions may cloud the relevant facts. Are you upset or too deeply involved to be objective? Are you frustrated, distracted, or too busy to discuss this right now? Are you making matters better or worse?

Being honest with ourselves can be tricky! Sometimes the complications may not be in our emotions, but in our thoughts. If our thinking process becomes dysfunctional, we compromise the likelihood of resolving conflict effectively.

Thinking Traps to Avoid

The *Halo Effect* demonstrates how our thoughts confuse logic and objectivity. It takes place when we allow someone's most obvious or endearing qualities to influence our decisions. Imagine a beautiful, scantily clad model appearing in a television commercial for lawn mowers. She may have absolutely no knowledge of lawn mowers and may never have used one, but because she is attractive, we assume she must have the professional insights to guide shoppers to the best lawn care supplies. Realistically, this kind of biased thinking may lead to an error in judgment.

Sometimes we compromise objectivity with the *I Still Remember Effect*. This tendency gives previous experiences more value than recent events. If you did me a favor several years ago, I still remain grateful and consider us to have a bond. If you hurt my feelings two years ago, the memory still causes me not to trust you today. This may be true despite repeated efforts to re-gain my trust. If my extended fishing trip causes me to arrive late for your brother's birthday party, but you tell me it is okay, it breaches our trust if you throw it in my face six months later!

A broken trust will remain broken until given the opportunity to heal. Sometimes a damaged relationship can be restored only by taking baby steps, but it will occur in the future, not the past. Sometimes you have to let it go, substituting the positive for the negative.

The opposite thinking trap is the *What Have You Done for Me (to Me) Lately Effect.* This kind of thinking blocks prior experiences, causing us to focus only on what has happened recently. Everyone knows a football coach is only as popular as his last game. We may have years of trust and good business relations, but a recent slip-up calls our entire relationship into question. A pastor may have served his congregation faithfully for many years, but recent critical comments suddenly challenge his effectiveness.

This type of dysfunctional thinking may cause us to forget that lasting relationships tend to develop through good times and bad, crisis, conflict and celebration. The result may be the loss of something or someone very precious.

Another dysfunctional thinking trap is *Overgeneralization*, such as using words like *always* and *never*. It also includes labeling. Labeling is judging someone as a Loser, Lady's Man or Moron, before you actually get to know him.

Mind Reading is a technique better left for gypsies and mediums. When we say things like, "You don't care" or "You don't love me," we put ourselves in the role of mind reader. In reality, we do not know if the other person cares or loves us. We can only say, "I don't feel loved." When I tell you what you think or how you feel, I am discounting your part of our relationship. I am prevented from hearing your words or understanding your perspective. I also force you to defend yourself, effectively escalating the conversation to a new intensity.

Sometimes we lock ourselves into a rigid thought process called *Dichotomous Thinking.* This fancy label refers to thinking that reduces a relationship and all its integral, intimate moments to all or nothing, success or dismal failure. It naively suggests a relationship must be perfect to be successful. If we argue over which sofa to buy or disagree over the color to paint the bedroom, we conclude our relationship will not work! We believe these minor disagreements will eventually lead to greater conflicts and our relationship will end in a flurry of expletives and gunfire. Actually, this creates a perverse simplification of our relationship and devalues our greater strengths and compatibilities. Life and relationships are not black and white: all or nothing. They have many diverse, beautiful colors that we should allow ourselves to enjoy!

It is also essential to avoid *personalizing* conflict. Some people really are idiots! They make incompetent business decisions, fail to utilize key members of their organization and cannot focus as you make your presentation. Some people are insensitive and say things that normal, socially competent people do not say. It is a mistake to take these conflicts personally or to exaggerate their importance. People do not easily change their behavior. In most cases, you have a better chance of controlling yours!

As soon as the conflict cycle has been broken, examine and accept what is happening with you. Bring it under control and then proceed to the next stage. Have you been focusing on the red things, while you should have been searching for blues, purples, yellows or greens?

EXPLORE

Explore the alternatives and opportunities available for resolution. Ask questions. Listen and understand. Jesus came upon a Samaritan woman at a local well (John 4:7-26). He asked for a drink and the woman said in a surprised tone, "How is it that you, a Jew, ask a drink of me, a woman of Samaria?" Since Jews and Samaritans did not socialize due to years of enmity, this was an unusual encounter.

In the next several exchanges, Jesus explored her life, her marital failures, her current living arrangement and her spiritual needs. He asked questions and shared his perspective on life and God. Eventually, she realized the spiritual possibilities offered by this gracious stranger.

During exploration, it is important to keep the conversation non-judgmental. Which statement creates less tension: "You hurt my feelings when you arrived fifteen minutes late for my birthday party" or "I was disappointed when my birthday party started and I didn't see you"? The latter statement tends to express my feelings without blaming you. When we use "I Statements," we allow ourselves to express what we feel or think, without applying guilt, blame or shame. This opens the gateway for improved communication.

Asking for help or clarification is another excellent exploring technique. Which inquiry creates less defensiveness: "How could you have made such a dumb mistake?" or "Help me understand why you took that approach"? Which inquiry is healthier for a relationship, "Why couldn't you be more careful?" or "Help me understand how you got the dent in the car fender"? When I ask you for help, I am inviting you to give me information - not defend your position. Eventually, I may need you to defend your position, if the issue is serious enough, but the questions I ask will have a considerable impact on our continuing relationship.

Exploration is an often overlooked part of the conflict resolution process. Usually, the old scripts, emotions and biased perspectives keep us from considering alternatives that may be outside the boat. The patience and interactions needed for exploration are also key ingredients in cultivating trust, which is a primary building block of close meaningful relationships.

RESPOND

Respond instead of reacting to conflict! Do not let a hasty reaction or an impulsive word crush a great relationship. Pause and give yourself some space. Review everything previously said and done. Acknowledge what you are thinking and feeling. Honestly accept responsibility for your part of the conflict. Explore the alternatives. Assemble the facts, feelings, perceptions and allegations to determine the most logical, reasonable, productive response. Be sure your words and behavior are the result of a well-chosen decision, not an emotional ill-conceived reaction. Be sure the words of your mouth and the meditation of your heart are acceptable in His sight!

EIGHTEEN

THE ANCIENT HILLS CONFLICT

The Ancient Hills Church represents a real church. Its smoldering conflict focused squarely on a small stone structure standing adjacent to its present sanctuary. The old building, constructed in the early nineteenth century, served as the small congregation's house of worship until the mid-twentieth century when the present sanctuary was built. Frontiersman, farmers and financiers had said their prayers and sang their hymns within its sacred walls.

Eventually, the old church became a local landmark, but the passing years were not kind. Its stuccoed walls were crumbling, its roof sinking and the cost of restoration prohibitive. Youth programs trying to use it as a respite from adult interference had come and gone. Ultimately, its increasing deterioration made it unsafe. After several failed renovation attempts, the question had finally reached a point of no return: What should be done with the old sanctuary?

TWO PERSPECTIVES

Previous ministers had found the issue too volatile and *avoidance* had been the prescribed strategy. The old building was hallowed ground for many. Decades of cherished memories draped its battered walls. The silent echoes of wedding vows and sacred hymns swirled through its exposed, sagging beams overhead. Its floor christened with tears of grief and spilled communion wine. Its poise atop a small hill, overlooking the shallow baptismal pool, now replaced by the modern indoor baptistery, still drew the attention of photographers and history enthusiasts. Its presence, though broken and hazardous, represented the congregation's heritage. Many, such as an elderly member who traced her ancestry back to the church's original commissioning in the late eighteenth century, refused to tolerate discussions of its demise. Her passion represented one congregational perspective. The removal or insensitive destruction of the old church promised to invoke explosive emotions within this group because they had the most to lose. Their heritage, memories and to a great extent their values, attached themselves to the old walls. They would not be bulldozed easily into the little pond.

Others saw the old building from a different perspective. They believed the church's mission should reach beyond itself, into the greater community. They saw the dirty old building as little more than a dilapidated eyesore in need of a significant and costly facelift or removal. The cost of renovation appeared staggering. They believed the congregation's modest treasury should be used to feed the hungry, heal the sick, shelter the homeless, and spread the Gospel, not to maintain an old relic.

THE PROCEEDINGS

During a cold Wednesday night in November, the motion was made. I had heard some talk about bringing the old church controversy, as it was known, to a vote. Many thought the issue had paralyzed the church long enough and it was time to move on or move back into the old building to suffocate with our memories. The motion established a committee to evaluate the condition of the old building and to bring a recommendation to restore or raze it once and for all! It received a second and passed after some brief discussion. The stage was set!

Responses were mixed. Some members caustically expressed an understandable, "Here we go again." Others trembled silently over what might happen if the building actually came down. The prospective vote threatened to resolve a controversy of biblical proportions through *competition*. This carried the potential for a congregational disaster! One side could lose, possibly a considerable part of themselves. The other might win little more than the privilege of seeing the issue decided and the building removed, while becoming the target for relentless criticism. Both sides would need a pastor without a label to help hold the pieces together.

Previously, *Accommodation* had also become a convenient conflict strategy. The old church controversy was the proverbial elephant in the room. Previous ministers discretely assigned members from both sides to various church committees, hoping to ensure a fair distribution of perspectives. Some members were not asked to serve with other members, because of lingering resentments from previous conflicts. One pastor said, "If Mr. Smith voted for a motion, Mr. Jones voted against it, just because Mr. Smith made the motion." Another former minister discovered the controversy had become symptomatic of interpersonal and inter-family conflicts from years past. The resulting power struggles were similar to those in private industry, family dynamics, or the local country club.

This lengthy and emotional controversy reached beyond the boundaries of stone and mortar. It challenged the little church to identify itself as a "Mission Oriented" or "Maintenance Oriented" congregation. Its identity and purpose were clenched tightly in the fist of conflict.

The more pressing issue was the appointment of an unbiased committee. After considerable prayer and assessment of the most controversial personalities, I appointed a committee of six. They were individuals expressing the most powerful attachment to each perspective. I though it wise to have them in the room arguing, rather than calling the shots from the parking lot!

By unanimous consent, the committee appointed me their Chairman, with full voting rights. This meant my vote could conceivably send the recommendation in one direction or the other. Realizing the perilous position in which I had been placed, I could see no alternative which would not result in a biased committee. I accepted.

The committee meetings were emotionally charged and rarely productive. After two months of discussions and a great deal of media attention from local newspaper and television outlets, we came to the congregation with no viable alternatives. Our solution was to ask the congregation to vote again. The most emotional issue for the non-restoration side was the use of the church treasury to fund the renovation. However, the restoration group needed funds to engage in the necessary due diligence. A *compromise* ballot was proposed:

> A Yes vote means that you will allow the church to seek a goal of $15,000 to be reached by June 30, 19--, at which point we shall apply for matching funds; if the goal is not met, the issue shall go back to committee for a final evaluation of the feasibility of the restoration plans.

> A No vote means that I want you to tear down the old church building and do not want to renovate.

I immediately saw flaws in this ballot. Both sides had a lot to lose. First, it allowed this matter to remain an open agenda for the next six months, which promised to weave serious complexities into the fabric of the church's mission and koinonia. Second, the goal itself suggested a potential threat. Suppose the committee raised $14,750. How intensely might the participants argue over the significance of the remaining $250 or even less? Would we really destroy the sacred, old building and the congregational unity because the goal was set a few dollars to high? Third, if the controversy went back to committee after six months, it might never be resolved. We would have accomplished little more than previous attempts. I believed *collaboration* offered the best solution, not compromise. We needed a less volatile, mutually acceptable solution.

The question needed to be open-ended and flexible, allowing the necessary time and resources to resolve a matter of this magnitude. After discussions with the congregational leadership, I proposed an alternative ballot, which I believed helped maintain the church's fellowship or koinonia. The following ballot was accepted by congregational vote:

> A Yes vote means I will support the efforts of a committee or individuals to secure funds to restore the old church building in the near future.

> A No vote means that I will not support any efforts to restore the old church building and I feel steps should be taken for its removal in the near future.

I realized the phrase *in the near future* was problematic, requiring interpretation. However, the restoration advocates did not want a specific date that might restrict potential progress. As long as they could bring the matter back for discussion if progress seemed to stall, the anti-restoration group agreed.

On the night of the final business session, the church seemed well attended for a Wednesday night service. Outside, a few men waited anxiously. They were smoking and discussing recent events, obviously trying to avoid uncomfortable emotions simmering beneath the surface. Inside, the atmosphere felt somber and thick with emotion. It seemed curiously reminiscent of the solemn moments just before a funeral service. A few ladies leaned over pew backs, whispering about the imminent vote. Some seemed absorbed in prayer. Others read their Bibles or jotted notes. An elderly lady sat motionless in her usual seat on the second row. A tear slowly trickled through the crevices of her tired, worn face, as she stared into the stained glass window. She seemed lost in time, searching, remembering, wondering. Even small children seemed drawn into the hallowed aura, sitting uncharacteristically quiet. The weight of our congregational identity balanced on this moment. I instructed all media outlets to remain outside. I called the meeting to order.

We approved seven absentee ballots according to the church bylaws and counted their votes. Previously, we agreed the time for discussion had passed. It was time to pray and vote. The congregation voted to restore the old sanctuary building by a sixty-three percent margin. A collective sigh of relief went up from both camps. No one wanted to fight. No one really wanted to see the old building destroyed. It was a matter of perspective.

Like a kid poking a sleeping bulldog, I refused to let it end. I had concerns over deciding such a long lasting, emotionally charged controversy with a sixty-three percent majority. Granted, the most volatile group had won, but this conflict could not be about winning. It had to be about reflecting the glory of God. I asked that we come back in ten days to vote again in hope of achieving a greater consensus. The church agreed.

As expected, the period between votes carried its own controversy. Two deacons, who supported the restoration perspective, came to my office. They said I had no authority to ask for a new vote. The following Sunday, I called an emergency Deacons' Meeting and confronted the issue. I did not identify the two visitors, since a personal confrontation served no productive purpose. I explained that as their pastor I had acted to preserve the integrity and fellowship of the church, hoping to avoid any further schism. I invited them to contradict me at the upcoming business meeting, but I received a strong vote of support and the matter was settled.

During the final business meeting, the congregation adopted a motion requiring a seventy per cent margin of victory to resolve the controversy. Church people talk. Even people on opposing sides shopped and worked together. Since the motion came from a strong advocate of the restoration group, I knew he had done his homework. Practically everyone knew the vote would confirm restoration and requiring a strong consensus made the decision more conclusive! Why get in their way? The final vote was seventy-seven per cent in favor of restoration. As we left the building, I told a friend I thought we were on solid ground since it takes a seventy-five per cent vote to remove a pastor!

I had less concern for the twenty-three per cent who lost the vote. All they wanted was for the restoration not to have an adverse impact on the church treasury. They got that. If the vote had been reversed, I would have faced a frightened, angry and significant minority, who likely would have been resistant to any form of new ministry for a great while. Instead, the restoration project was given new life, with the promise of time and resources to accomplish their objective. The conflict was resolved and both sides achieved their primary goal.

THE AFTERMATH

Following the final vote, the congregation formed another committee empowered to pursue renovation of the old church building. Since that time, the dirty, broken stucco façade has been removed, exposing a beautiful stone sanctuary. A board of directors has been established to oversee the project, with participants coming from both original perspectives. Neither side in the conflict perceived themselves as losers.

Both sides gained a lasting memorial to their heritage and Christian perseverance.

I have often wondered how I might have handled the situation had the vote been reversed. Influential and generous church leaders may have left or resisted new ministry opportunities. I may have been assigned blame for perceived miss-steps. I cannot bring myself to imagine the emotional turbulence that may have erupted from our little hill on the day bulldozers pushed the old building into the pond. Fortunately, we used a sound conflict resolution strategy. We also employed Paul's advice to the Philippians:

> *So if there is any encouragement in Christ, any incentive of love, any participation in the Spirit, any affection and sympathy, complete my joy by being of the same mind, having the same love, being in full accord and of one mind. Do nothing from selfishness or conceit, but in humility count others better than yourselves. Let each of you look not only to his own interests but also to the interests of others (2:1-4).*

NINETEEN

STICKS AND STONES

The sound of crying pulled me from my sleep and into my daughter's bedroom. The room was softly illuminated by lights from the church sanctuary just outside. Megan was still asleep, but Kirsti had apparently awakened from a bad dream. As I knelt beside her bed, my innocent, five-year-old daughter put both arms around my neck and said, "Daddy, I don't want to go to church anymore."

The experts say there are no difficult people, only difficult behavior. It is my perspective that there are indeed difficult people. I have met them, spoken to them and felt the indiscriminant power of their unkindness. Even my little girl recognized difficult people when she saw them!

Pastors generally try not to bring problems home, especially where impressionable little girls can hear. However, Kirsti had obviously heard conversations and perceived the tensions caused by recent events at church. Her disturbing dream caused me to realize how deeply the tentacles of conflict can reach.

Sometimes even the best intentions are met with defiant, difficult behavior. We are left searching in vain for the appropriate words or paralyzed with emotions. No one has the correct answer for every situation, but a few tips my help along the way.

DO NOT TAKE IT PERSONALLY

Conflict means to strike, but unless the blow is literal, try not to take it personally. Difficult people may be angry, afraid, anxious, insecure or generally obnoxious. However, this says more about them than you. When confronted by difficult people, focus on their behavior.

Difficult people are generally people with whom we have trouble communicating or building a relationship. These differences may be caused by age, gender, or ethnicity. However, they may also result from differing perspectives. You may think your tenant should pay his rent on time. He may think he deserves a grace period at the beginning of each month. This may be annoying, but it is not personal.

When King David arrived in Bahurim, Shimei, a relative of his old adversary King Saul, greeted him (2 Samuel 16:5-14). Apparently, he did not like King David and cursed him continually. He threw rocks at him. He even threw handfuls of dirt. One of the king's soldiers generously offered to behead the guy and silence his taunts, but David showed better discretion. He said, "Leave him alone and let him curse." Perhaps this is the origin of "Sticks and stones...." King David did not take the insults or hostile behavior personally. Even as he and his entourage left town, Shimei ran along beside him cursing and throwing rocks. But David remained unaffected. He arrived at his destination unscathed and refreshed himself.

DRAW THEM INTO YOUR WORLD

Angry, aggressive people prefer to draw us into their angry, aggressive world. This is a place where arguments and antagonisms are plentiful. It is where they are more comfortable. Instead of following them down some winding pathway into their brooding aggression, stay calm and do not debate or argue. If they become loud and argumentative, soften your voice and seek out areas of agreement, even if only minor. Stay on task and control your response. If you refuse to argue, they may abruptly hang up or leave, smugly carrying their hostility towards some other unsuspecting target.

Other people may not intend to be difficult. They may be afraid, anxious, or uncertain how to express themselves effectively. Do not be intimidated or annoyed by silence. Calmly draw them also into your world by rephrasing their comments with less toxic statements. If a parent says, "My son's room is a pigsty!" you might respond, "He certainly has a unique perspective on tidiness. What do you need him to do?" If someone insists, "It's my way or the highway," you might respond, "Your way is certainly a great alternative! Is it possible we may have overlooked something?" When you are in conflict with difficult people, you need to be in your world, not theirs. Invite them in and help them feel welcome.

LEARN TO SAY NO

Generally, time share salesmen, telemarketers and used car salesmen are perceived as difficult. As they work harder, talk faster and become more persistent, the more difficult they seem. How do we tell them *No*? We want people to like us.

When situations require us to say *No* to someone who depends on us, the resulting emotion is usually guilt. We do not like to disappoint people, especially those who love us. Sometimes we even feel a twinge of guilt when declining the telemarketer. However, we say *No* more often than it appears.

Time is a finite commodity. A year consists of three hundred sixty-five days. Each day consists of only twenty-four hours. These facts are non-negotiable! If I agree to spend three hours a day on your project, I am effectively saying I will not spend those same three hours on any other activity. If I agree to work late every night this week, I am saying I will not be home with my family. If I agree to serve on your committee, I will not have an equal amount of time to do other things I might rather do. Consequently, we might as well be selective.

When facing a situation or offer you want to decline, give yourself permission to say, "No." Go ahead and try it! Take a deep breath, remain calm, be honest and avoid euphemisms like, "Not right now," "This doesn't seem right," or "Maybe some other time." Say "No" and stick to it. After each new proposal, give the same answer. If possible, indicate what you may be willing to do as an alternative, but let yourself off the hook. The guilt you feel is often self-imposed and unnecessary.

As you become more comfortable with saying "No", you may feel fewer discontentments when you say "Yes."

KNOW WHERE TO DRAW THE LINE

Primum nil nocere is a fundamental principle in emergency medicine. It means, first, do no harm. Do not make matters worse! Sometimes conflict becomes intense. Emotions flare, inexcusable or inappropriate things are said, and assertiveness becomes aggression or rage. At these times, it is wise to acknowledge your limitations and your circumstances. If you can no longer engage in a reasonable dialogue or perceive yourself threatened, do not make it worse. Allow yourself to step away. Hang up the phone, politely excuse yourself from the room, or ask that the conversation be continued at another time. A fine line exists between avoidance and discerned withdrawal, but safety is always paramount.

Drawing the line may be tricky. Do not draw a line in the sand, issuing an ultimatum, such as, "One more word and I'll hang up!" This transitions the conversation from the original topic to a show-down! It is also unwise to turn your back abruptly and walk away from a heated discussion, although walking away may be appropriate. Try to disengage, without appearing to dismiss the aggressive party. If appropriate and possible, use the *Twenty Minute* time-out technique for allowing emotions to cool.

Some people are offended by profanity. Others, who possibly grew up in an environment where profanity was familiar vocabulary, may unintentionally complicate conflict. Before you hang up, walk away or draw the wrong conclusion about this person, check out your perception. Ask for clarification. Something as simple as "Excuse me, but I feel uncomfortable with your choice of words," may open the door to better dialogue.

RESPOND WITH GRACE

The one thing we can control in conflict is ourselves! Angry people are angry for a reason far beyond your control. Resentful people, demanding people, obnoxious people, complainers and victims have become who they are through a lifetime of experiences. You did not break them and you likely cannot fix them! You can only control your response to them.

Difficult people and their difficult behavior deserve to be confronted. Their behavior practically invites a justified rebuke. However, Jesus said, "A new commandment I give to you, that you love one another, even as I have loved you." Even though the confrontation and rebuke are justified, they should be administered with appropriate discretion.

Asking us to love difficult people seems a little naïve, until we remember it is their behavior making them so hard to love. Their behavior makes us feel uncomfortable. It creates unpleasant circumstances that run havoc with our emotions and cause physical distress. We do not like it! However, the strength to endure and to respond graciously to these transgressors is woven into the fabric of our faith in God. Jesus said, "I am the vine, you are the branches. He who abides in me and I in him, he it is that bears much fruit, apart from me you can do nothing." Paul later affirmed that statement from his conflicted spiritual life when he wrote, "I can do all things in him who strengthens me."

TWENTY

CALCULATED FORGIVENESS?

The most egregious example of interpersonal conflict I have ever witnessed, beyond violence or physical abuse, comes from the story of a divorced father and his two daughters. An extra-marital affair led to vile hostilities between the husband and wife. Ultimately a mean- spirited divorce resulted. The sinful father moved into an apartment, continuing to see his young daughters on weekends. The mother remained captive to seething emotions and insecurities. She lived in a world saturated in blame and victimization, but void of self-awareness. Eventually, consumed in bitterness, she told her twelve year-old daughter the sordid details of the events leading up to the divorce. This was apparently more information than the child could comprehend or emotionally cope.

One afternoon, just after Father's Day, the daughter and her father had a pleasant lunch near his office. Afterwards, with no explanation, she silently ended their relationship. When he went to their house for clarification, the mother said the child did not want to talk with him. When he called, she said the same. The father continued sending birthday cards, Christmas gifts and letters, apologizing for sins of commission and omission, but he could never be sure she received them. Checks were not cashed. Letters were not answered. Ten years passed and they did not speak again. He replayed their last conversation a thousand times in his mind, never finding a clue to explain what triggered her abrupt, uncharacteristic behavior.

Each night, without exception, the heartbroken father prayed for his daughter to love him again. He prayed to again hear her playful laugher, to see her smile, to hold her hand. Finally, after learning from a third party that his daughter had married, the cards and the prayers stopped. At that moment, a part of his anguished soul finally died.

This father committed a sin against God, his wife and his children. He pleaded for God's forgiveness and theirs. Yet, forgiveness did not come. His guilt became an irreconcilable shame, tormenting his dreams. Joy was a forgotten commodity. His cherished daughter became little more than tortured memories drawn from a deepening pool of tears. He symbolically linked God's forgiveness with that of his daughter's. It is a forgiveness that may never come.

Perhaps the sinful father deserves never to be forgiven! I imagine he agrees with that statement. Certainly his ex-wife agrees and with the passing of time, their daughters appear to agree. Tragically, he also believes God agrees.

However, God took something as wicked, brutal, and unholy as the crucifixion of his only begotten son and created Easter. From Garden of Eden, to David's sin with Bathsheba, to Saul's persecution of the Christians, and for sinful individuals throughout the pages of the New Testament, God responded with an unexpected and frequently undeserved grace. Fortunately, God's forgiveness is not linked to a daughter's love, forgiveness, maturity or distorted frame of reference.

Eventually, this troubled father may become reconciled to God, but he may never experience his treasured daughter's love again. However, the effective resolution of relationship conflict generally requires some degree of forgiveness. Hopefully, the offended daughter will realize the intrinsic value of having a father who loves her dearly and the importance of being something more than a surrogate of her mother's revenge.

However, sometimes even forgiveness is not really forgiveness. The disciple Peter asked Jesus, "Lord, how often shall my brother sin against me, and I forgive him? As many as seven times?" (Matt. 18:21-22). I often wondered if Peter's brother already had six strikes against him! Clearly, Peter was looking for a biblical calculation for forgiveness. The question beyond the question was asking, "When do I get to strike back?" Jesus answered, "Seventy times seven," meaning genuine forgiveness is beyond calculation. Anything less is only fair warning!

Jesus forgave people all the time. He forgave people lying on sick beds, being lowered through ceilings, climbing in trees and drawing water from wells. He forgave people at the temple, dinner parties and even while nailed to the cross. He forgave people who arrested him, beat him, doubted and denied him. He even told stories about forgiveness. But Peter needed a number! Sometimes we all do.

Do you recall the story of King David and Shimei (2 Samuel16:5-14)? Shimei was a relative of King Saul, who did not like it that David had become the new king. He called him names. He said David was "a worthless fellow" and a "Man of Blood." In righteous indignation, Shimei said "The Lord has avenged upon you all the blood of the house of Saul, in whose place you have reigned." As the king and his entourage passed through town, Shimei cursed, threw rocks and even handfuls of dirt. When one of his military leaders offered to dispose of the annoying villager, King David said to leave him alone with this curses. It seemed the response you might expect from a spiritual leader, who wrote such beautiful psalms. Unfortunately, the story does not end there.

After Shimei had some time to think about his behavior, he realized he had acted inappropriately. Grown men do not curse and throw rocks at kings, or anyone else for that matter. He brought more than a thousand men and servants to the Jordan River to pay homage to King David. Shimei fell down before the king and begged for forgiveness (2 Samuel 19:16-23).

Once again, a soldier offered to kill Shimei for his previous transgressions. David again intervened, saying to Shimei, "You shall not die." It appeared Shimei's apology had touched the king's heart. The relationship conflict had been resolved. However, appearances can be deceiving.

David may have been the *Lord's Anointed* and King of Israel, but he was also human! He really did not like Shimei or the disrespectful way he mocked him. As the king was about to die, he called for his son Solomon (1Kings 2:1-9). He charged Solomon to be strong, to prove himself a man, to walk in the ways of God and to follow the statutes, commandments, ordinances and testimonies of God as written in the

Law of Moses. Then, in a conversation that could have come from the pages of a Mario Puzo novel, King David gave Solomon a list of adversaries he needed to eliminate. His hit list included Shimei.

In a marvelous twist of semantics, King David said, "Now I swore an oath that I wouldn't kill him, but you're a *wise man*. You know what you ought to do to him. Bring his gray head down with blood." The king had forgiven Shimei, but only while it was politically advantageous. King David's peaceful relationship with Shimei had been a selfish deception. Now, it seemed of little value to keep Shimei alive, especially since he might be a threat to Solomon's reign. This great man, who played soothing music and wrote beautiful poems, went to his grave whispering words of revenge. How many times should he have forgiven his brother?

Sometimes it is hard to let go of things like anger, betrayal, or deception. We may even think we have moved on, and then years later, realize the emotions still linger just beneath the surface. Like a sterile, scarred pathway in the yard, worn by an angry dog pulling at the end of his chain, our soul is disfigured by the relentless emotions. We become calloused and desensitized by their constant presence. When couples divorce over issues like adultery, leaving their pain indelibly etched into the innocent faces of their children, genuine forgiveness is often sacrificed to the omnipresent god of acrimony. However, even in these intensely conflicted relationships, I believe God expects us to follow Jesus' model.

Following the Last Supper, on their way into the Garden of Gethsemane, Jesus and Peter had a quiet conversation about the coming events. Peter declared his uncompromised commitment to Jesus, pledging never to fail him. Jesus sadly informed Peter he would soon deny even knowing him, not once, but three times.

As the pungent words of his third denial slipped through his lips, Peter's emotions became overwhelming. He wept bitterly. Undoubtedly, he recalled Jesus' prophetic words, in the face of his haughty protests. I think he also reflected on the depth of their relationship. Perhaps, he remembered the day Jesus called him from his fishing boat to become a disciple. Maybe he recalled the night on the lake, when he tried to walk on water and Jesus had to catch him as he went under. He possibly recalled only a short time earlier, when Jesus asked him to watch and wait in the Garden of Gethsemane, but he kept falling asleep. I believe Peter's psychological guilt was traveling down a dark, treacherous road to spiritual shame. How many times should he be forgiven?

Following the resurrection, Peter, Thomas, Nathaniel and a few others decided to go night fishing in the Sea of Tiberias (John 21:1-19). They were not having any luck, until Jesus arrived and told them where to find the best fishing spots. By breakfast time, they had more than a hundred and fifty fish. As they sat around the fire, eating S'mores and the last few morsels of fried fish, Jesus asked Peter, "Do you love me more than these?" It is hard to say whether Jesus referred to the other disciples, his fishing gear, or the fish they just had for breakfast, but that did not matter. Peter knew what he was really asking. He still remembered the night Jesus was arrested. Peter said, "Yes, Lord, you know that I love you." Jesus asked Peter two more times if he loved him. Peter affirmed his love three times: once for each denial. Perhaps, when he answered the third time, Peter realized how many times he should forgive his brother.

Peter must have been the kind of person who perceives the world through the senses. When he asked Jesus how many times he should forgive his brother, he needed a number. He needed a rule. He needed specifics. Jesus was smart enough to understand Peter's personality and chose to communicate forgiveness in terms he would understand.

Peter had denied Jesus three times and the shame was unbearable. So, Jesus asked him three times if he loved him. Peter affirmed his love three times and finally understood. The answer to the question, "How many times shall I forgive my brother who sins against me?" is not three or seven or seventy-times seven. It is not a number. It is every time!

Jesus forgave people he met on the streets and hillsides, the soldiers who beat and crucified him, and his friend Simon Peter, who disgracefully denied knowing him. He gives us a model to follow as we endure the many conflicts in our daily lives. He invites us to forgive the rude driver who causes us to slam on brakes and spill our coffee. He encourages us to forgive the narcissistic boss, the incompetent supervisor, the rude co-worker, even the defiant daughter-in-law with another box of tape recorders and a sinful husband. He demonstrates how to forgive those who mortally wound our most intimate relationships and defile our most sacred commitments. He firmly insists that only he or she who is without sin may cast the first stone. Then, he speaks to our hearts in a gentle, graceful and collective whisper, "Go, and sin no more."

As the Children of Israel wandered the wilderness in search of the Promised Land, they were much like you and me. We wander through the wilderness of each day, sometimes embittered by the residual scars of our shackles, encountering disappointments, confusion, frustration, sometimes wild beasts and conflicts of all sorts. Yet, our search is also for a Promised Land, where we are genuinely reconciled with our brothers and sisters, co-workers, neighbors, parents, spouse and children. As we journey through life, encountering uncharted emotions, troubling thoughts and unexpected conflict, sometimes with those whom we love the most, we are reminded of God's daily presence in our lives. We are tenderly caressed by an ancient blessing that transcends time, culture and sophistication:

> *The Lord bless you and keep you. The Lord make his face to shine upon you and be gracious to you: the Lord lift up his countenance upon you, and give you peace, both now and forever more. Amen*

ENDNOTES

1 For a synopsis of Gov. Mark Sanford's scandal and subsequent events see "The Scandal: Sanford leaves constituents cold", by John O'Connor, October 4, 2009, *The State* newspaper, Columbia, SC.

2 Kenneth R. Norris, *In Need of A Deacon*, The Deacon, The Sunday School Board of the Southern Baptist Convention, Nashville, TN. Oct-Dec, 1987:41-43. Used by Permission of LifeWay Christian Resources.

3 *Two and a Half Men*, Chuck Lorre Productions, The Tannenbaum Company, Warner Brothers Television, Performances by Charlie Sheen, Jon Cryer, Angus T. Jones, 2003-2010.

4 *The Big Bang Theory*, Chuck Lorre Productions, Warner Brothers Television, Performances by Jim Parsons, Johnny Galecki, Kaley Cuoco , 2007-2010

5 This discussion of personality tendencies uses concepts expressed by Karl Jung and incorporated into the Myers-Briggs Personality Inventory by Isabel Myers and Katherine Briggs. An excellent resource for further discussion is *Gifts Differing: Understanding Personality Types* by Isabel Briggs Myers and Peter B. Myers: Davies-Black Publishing, Mountain View, California, 1980.

6 *Frasier*, David Angell, Peter Casey, David Lee (Grub Street Productions), Grammnet Productions and Paramount Television, Performances by Kelsey Grammer, David Hyde Peirce, John Mahoney, Jane Leeves, Peri Gilpin, 1993-2004.

[7] Kenneth R. Norris, *Don't Eat Soup with Your Fingers*, <u>Church Administration Magazine</u>, The Sunday School Board of the Southern Baptist Convention, Nashville, TN. January 1994: 36-38. Used by permission of LifeWay Christian Resources.

[8] *American Idol*, Created by Simon Fuller, Produced by 19 TV Limited & Fremantlemedia North America, Inc., 2002-2010.